COLD WAR
EAST ANGLIA

COLD WAR
EAST ANGLIA

JIM WILSON OBE

To Judith, for her love, support and understanding

First published 2014

The History Press
The Mill, Brimscombe Port
Stroud, Gloucestershire, GL5 2QG
www.thehistorypress.co.uk

British Library Cataloguing in Publication Data.
A catalogue record for this book is available from the British Library.

ISBN 978 0 7509 5638 3

Typesetting and origination by The History Press
Printed in Great Britain

CONTENTS

FOREWORD

THE IMPACT ON East Anglia of the 'friendly invasion' by the United States Army Air Force in the 1940s left a huge legacy which remains alive seventy years on. In many ways, the impact of the Cold War had a similar social and cultural impact on East Anglia. The region was a great deal more vulnerable to the potential horror of nuclear attack than those who lived through decades of nuclear tension probably realised.

East Anglia hosted the full range of Cold War sites. It was the launch pad for both the UK and America's first response had the Soviet Union mounted a pre-emptive strike, as appeared frighteningly possible, particularly in the 1950s and 1960s. Certainly, East Anglia was in the cross-hairs of the USSR's nuclear trigger – so many strategic targets were located in the region.

There is a growing realisation that the legacy of the Cold War in the region should be preserved in order that future generations can appreciate how it affected life in East Anglia. So much has already been lost, or is under threat, and preservation is an urgent issue. English Heritage is undertaking to save some of East Anglia's iconic Cold War buildings and the National Trust has given protection to buildings at Orford Ness which were involved in the development of the UK's first nuclear weapons, but much more remains to be done.

A measure towards preserving the legacy of the Cold War years is the study being undertaken by the University of East Anglia's Centre of East Anglian Studies, funded by a grant from the Arts and Humanities Research Council. Much of the historical research into the Cold War has concentrated on high-level policy-making and military strategy. The UEA project hopes to focus more on the Cold War at a community level. As the outline statement of the project states:

> The scale, significance and, most importantly, the impact of the gradual and rather secretive militarisation of the region in the period remains largely unchartered. This is a consequence of the secrecy of the Cold War itself, but also because the focus of the historians has been on the global Cold War, rather than the Cold War as fought at a local level. The front line of this 'secret' war lay in the heart of Britain's regional communities, both rural – where nuclear weapons sites, listening stations, airbases and laboratories sprang up next to small villages and at the end of leafy lanes – and urban, where the rapidly expanding armaments industry drove the development of new towns. The consequence of this involvement was that villages and small towns across the nation faced the prospect of devastation at the hands of Soviet nuclear and conventional weapons that was unprecedented, even during the Second World War.

As we approach the 25th anniversary of the fall of the Berlin Wall, and the subsequent end of the Cold War, this book is a contribution to recording some of the aspects of the Cold War in East Anglia told, for the most part, through the voices of people who were closely involved.

Jim Wilson OBE, 2014

ACKNOWLEDGEMENTS

I AM GRATEFUL to a number of people who have trawled their memories, in some cases almost as far back as sixty years, to recall their experiences in the early days of the Cold War, and how if the temperature of international relations suddenly worsened East Anglia would have faced up to nuclear conflict.

I am indebted in particular to Mike Allisstone, Wayne Cocroft, John Cogdale, Huby Fairhead, Roland Hall, David Heading, Leonard Hewitt, Tony Howells, Justyn Keeble, David Morris, Arthur Nichols, Peter Portanova, Ron Randell, Stuart Robathan, Bob Rudasill, Harry Teague MBE, Sam Tolley, Denis Tuttle and David Twyford.

I particularly want to thank Keith and Margot Eldred, owners of the former Barnham nuclear bomb store, now an industrial estate, where the UK's first 'Blue Danube' nuclear weapons were stored and maintained in the late 1950s and early 1960s, in utmost secrecy. In conjunction with English Heritage, they are now ensuring that this unique memorial to the Cold War is preserved and kept as a historic reminder of those early threatening years of Cold War confrontation.

GLOSSARY

ADOC – Air Defence Operations Centre
AFB – Air Force Base (USAF)
AFC – Air Force Cross
AWRE – Atomic Weapons Research Establishment
BCAS – Bomber Command Armament School
BMEWS – Ballistic Missiles Early Warning System
BPI – Bomb Power Indicator
CDEE – Chemical Defence Experimental Establishment
C-in-C – Commander-in-Chief
CND – Campaign for Nuclear Disarmament
CRE – Central Reconnaissance Establishment
DERA – Defence Evaluation and Research Agency
DFC – Distinguished Flying Cross
EBI – Extended Background Investigation
ELINT – Electronic Intelligence
Flt Lt – Flight Lieutenant
Flt Sgt – Flight Sergeant
FOIA – Freedom of Information Act
FP – Fluorescent Particles
GCHQ – Government Communications Headquarters
GZI – Ground Zero Indicator
HEROD – High Explosives Research Operational Distribution
IRBM – Intermediate Range Ballistic Missile

JIC – Joint Intelligence Committee
JIGSAW – Joint Inter-Services Group for the Study of All-Out War
Lt Col – Lieutenant Colonel
MT – Mechanical Transport
NATO – North Atlantic Treaty Organisation
NBC – Nuclear, Biological and Chemical
PM – Prime Minister
PRO – Public Records Office
PRP – Personnel Reliability Program
PV – Positive Vetting
QRA – Quick Readiness Alert
RAF – Royal Air Force
ROC – Royal Observer Corps
RSG – Regional Seat of Government
RSM – Radiac Survey Meter
SAC – Strategic Air Command
SACEUR – Supreme Allied Commander Europe
SALT – Strategic Arms Limitations Treaties
SDI – Strategic Defense Initiative
Sgt – Sergeant
SIOP – Single Integrated Operational Plan
Sqn Ldr – Squadron Leader
SW – Special Weapon
TEL – Transporter Erector Launcher
TNA – The National Archive
Wg Cdr – Wing Commander
UEA – University of East Anglia
UFO – Unidentified Flying Object
UKWMO – UK Warning and Monitoring Organisation
USAF – United States Air Force
USSR – Union of Soviet Socialist Republics

INTRODUCTION

> We must not forget that by creating the American atomic base in East Anglia, we have made ourselves the target, and perhaps the bull's eye of a Soviet attack.
>
> *Winston Churchill, 15 February 1951.*[1]

It is a quarter of a century since the fall of the Berlin Wall, which led to the end of the Cold War. A whole generation has grown up without experiencing the dread and anxiety of Cold War. Looking back over twenty-five years it is hard to recapture the mood that prevailed during those nervous Cold War years. We lived, particularly when tensions were highest, under a threat of nuclear annihilation, mutually assured destruction, the iconic four-minute warning, and a reliance on the protective power of a credible 'deterrence'. Even though 'Protect & Survive' leaflets handed out by the government were widely derided, we had to believe official inferences that nuclear war was 'survivable'. But declassified documents from the 'secret state' now prove that the effort to sustain public morale took precedence over the much gloomier forecasts produced by experts and scientists in Whitehall, which bore rather more relevance to reality. Deep in Whitehall, civil servants of the JIGSAW Group (Joint Inter-Services Group for the Study of All-Out War) were discussing the point at which a nation state would pass beyond any hope of revival and reach the stage of total breakdown.[2]

It was impossible to grasp the awfulness of what could happen. To have morbidly dwelt upon it would have made normal life through four decades almost impossible. So we all got on with our lives, pushing to the back of our minds the spectre of the possibility that the Cold War would heat up.

Yet every day, on both sides of the Iron Curtain, the military prepared themselves to strike back with incalculable nuclear force. It was their job to think about and act out the unthinkable. If deterrence was to work – and thank God it did – the UK and its allies had to have the capability, and the political will, to deliver an overwhelming nuclear strike whatever the cost. 'Quick Readiness Alert' (QRA), to achieve just that, was practised daily on airbases across East Anglia, both British and American. Unimaginable nuclear strike power was available in the region to respond at less than fifteen minutes' notice, twenty-four hours a day and 365 days a year.

From January 1962, on operational V-bomber bases across the region, one aircraft per squadron was sitting on the runway around the clock, armed with a nuclear weapon, its crew ready to take off within fifteen minutes or less. The destructive power aboard each bomber was equal to all the bombs dropped on Nazi Germany in the whole of the Second World War. As one senior Whitehall mandarin, Sir Kevin Tebbit, who as Permanent Secretary at the Ministry of Defence was close to war planning, and privy to the secret fears debated in Whitehall, recalled: 'Hardly anyone died in the Cold War, but we lived on a daily basis with the risk that everyone might ...'[3]

Nowhere in Britain was that comment more true than in East Anglia, as Winston Churchill, in his 1951 speech, recognised. As was so often proved, Churchill's opinion was prescient. Harold Macmillan, who became prime minister in 1956, repeated Churchill's assertion. When he signed the agreement with President Eisenhower to base American nuclear-tipped missiles on launch pads in East Anglia, he told a press conference that he was well aware the decision would make us the free world's first nuclear attack target. 'We can't help that,' he said, adding that if the missiles were ever fired it would mean the failure of all the purposes for which they were devised.[4]

East Anglia's vulnerability was reinforced again in 1958, the year those first Norfolk Thor nuclear missiles became operational. A secret government paper presented to ministers made clear that: 'The Russians, either using bombers or ballistic missiles when available, could mount a comprehensive attack on this country. It would be aimed in all probability at nuclear bomber bases [there were many in East Anglia] and offensive missile launching sites [again based largely in East Anglia], a total of 40 or 50 sites as a first priority ...'[5] The paper went on to say that even if there were no deliberate attacks on large centres of population, the size of the UK and the possibility of weapons going astray made it likely that towns and cities would be hit. If, as was expected, ground burst weapons were used, extensive areas of the country would be contaminated by fallout. A grim prospect, but of course the public were never told, for fear that morale would be destroyed.

There was also Macmillan's rather blasé comment in his personal diary at the time of the Cuban crisis in October 1962: 'To us who face 500 of these missiles in Russia trained on Europe there is something slightly ironical about these 20 or so in Cuba. But, as I told the President, when one lives on Vesuvius, one takes little account of the risk of explosions.' For those of us living in East Anglia, Vesuvius was too close to home for comfort![6]

While weapons, and the means to deliver them, developed and improved in their destructive power, in the frenzy of the arms race East Anglia grew more prominent as the 'bull's eye' of the USSR's UK target. The region was peppered with strategic bases. A nuclear world war – effectively a Third World War – would have seen the Soviets attempt to destroy them, if only to ensure their own survival.

East Anglia was home, during the Cold War years, to massive British and American nuclear force. It hosted the launch pads for the first operational nuclear ballistic missiles deployed in the West; the UK's first generation of nuclear bombs were stored under armed guard and in considerable secrecy on the Norfolk/Suffolk border; the UK's arsenal of early nuclear weapons was put through crucial ballistic and environmental tests at the Aldermaston Nuclear Research Establishment's offshoot in Suffolk; and East Anglia was home to radar early warning sites scanning the skies for Soviet intruders. Fighter aircraft and surface to air missile batteries were poised on East Anglian bases to deter Soviet aircraft from approaching UK airspace. Risky spy flights over Soviet territory were launched from regional airfields, and there was probably much more from which the veil of secrecy remains to be lifted. No wonder the Soviets mapped East Anglia in some detail.

It is only now that national organisations set up to preserve our heritage are realising that something needs to be done to secure what is left of Britain's tangible Cold War legacy before it is lost. Sadly, much has already gone. English Heritage and the National Trust have both taken steps to ensure that some of the iconic buildings in the region are protected so that future generations can appreciate what the Cold War meant to those who lived through it, the impact it had on East Anglia, and the significance of the Cold War in the region's, and the country's, history.

East Anglia played a remarkable pioneering role in the introduction of the UK's nuclear deterrent, which held the balance of power and was the basis of bluff and counter-bluff between two opposing ideologies. The RAF's armaments training school, from which nuclear weapons were first introduced into the V-Force, was based at Wittering in Cambridgeshire. Feltwell in Norfolk became the RAF's ballistic missile training school. At Barnham, on the Norfolk/Suffolk border, the UK's first nuclear bombs and their fissile cores were stored and serviced. Orford Ness, on the Suffolk coast, was the focus of tests crucial to the credibility of the UK's nuclear strength. Elsewhere in Norfolk, Suffolk and Cambridgeshire, British and American deterrent forces were deployed operationally.

Before Polaris-armed submarines took over the main nuclear deterrent role, the UK's nuclear armoury relied on the 'V-Force' and the 'Thor' missile force which were extensively based in the region. In a very real sense, East Anglia was the front line for the defence of Europe.

It was also America's first line of resistance or attack. Until the USA managed to develop intercontinental ballistic missiles which could be fired from silos on the American mainland, nuclear armed missiles on East Anglian launch pads would constitute a powerful element of America, and the West's, initial strike force. East Anglia hosted America's first means of defence. The region was where America's first overseas stores of nuclear bombs were located. As early as June 1950, just after the Korean War had broken out, President Truman approved the transfer of eighty-nine atomic bombs to bases in East Anglia. As the military director of the Manhattan Project, General Leslie Groves, put it: 'If there are to be atomic bombs in the world we [America] must have the best, the biggest, and the most.'[7] All this added up, undisputedly, to East Anglia being Churchill's 'bull's eye'.

In the Cold War's early years, before the Berlin Airlift, the US Joint Chiefs of Staff approved America's first nuclear age war plan directed at the Soviet Union, code named 'Halfmoon'. It assumed that war would start in Europe and, because the Soviet Union had greater strength in manpower and conventional warfare, the United States would rapidly lose a series of crucial land battles. Unable to hold Western Germany, the US Army would be forced to fight a retreat across Europe to seaports in France and Italy where, in operations reminiscent of Dunkirk, they would be evacuated by the American Navy. Fifteen days after the first shots had been fired America would launch a counter-attack from airbases in East Anglia, dropping up to 133 atomic bombs aimed at seventy Soviet cities. Pentagon officials warned the American Chiefs of Staff that the Soviet response would be 'a devastating, annihilating' nuclear counter-attack on the UK. East Anglian airbases would be the first destroyed. Denied 'front-line' bases close to continental Europe,

America would be forced to use bases in Egypt, Iceland, Greenland or Alaska from which to continue their nuclear attack.

But a strike from Russia was not the only nuclear threat East Anglian towns and villages faced. The reliability of the electronic, mechanical and explosive components of America's early nuclear bombs was uncertain, and US experts were fearful a nuclear bomber crash during take-off would pose a substantial risk to a large area in the vicinity of one of America's Norfolk or Suffolk airbases.

The Mark 3 bomb was labelled by experts too dangerous to be flown in its fully assembled state over American territory. However, the US Strategic Air Command put no such safety restrictions on the Mark 3 being flown over British soil. Facilities to assemble the bombs were secretly built at Sculthorpe and Lakenheath. Should war occur, the intention was for American B-29s to fly from the States to East Anglia with partially assembled Mark 3s. At Sculthorpe and Lakenheath the plutonium cores would be inserted and then the B-29s would take off and head for their targets in the Soviet Union. If one of the bombers crashed during take-off, and the B-29 was notorious among pilots for its handling problems, the RAF base and neighbouring East Anglian towns and villages stood a high risk of obliteration.

Recognising that this was a real possibility, the Americans looked for widely spread sites in the countryside of Norfolk and Suffolk where atom bombs could be stored, on the basis that if one exploded others in storage would survive. This was particularly true when US authorities decided that to store the bombs in the UK without their nuclear cores would mean an unacceptable delay in mounting an offensive operation in a real emergency, so the cores too were sent for storage alongside the bombs on regional bases.

The electrical system of the Mark 3 was powered by a car battery. To change it, the weapon had to be largely taken apart. Its plutonium core radiated so much heat that if it was left in the bomb for too long it would start to melt the weapon's delicate explosive lenses. Assembling the weapon was hazardous; a stray wire, a spark caused by static electricity, or an inadvertent human error could have ended in disaster.

By 1950, some of these hazards to East Anglian populations were marginally reduced. America's Mark 4 implosion bomb was in full-scale production. It was much safer than previous designs, could be assembled in two hours, and incorporated a number of features to prevent premature detonation. Its nuclear core was stored in the aircraft's cockpit and inserted through a trap door into the bomb in mid-flight. As long as the core was kept physically separate from the rest of the bomb it was impossible for a plane crash to cause a nuclear explosion.

When, in 1949, the Soviet Union announced that it too was a nuclear power, the consequences for the UK were clear. There was now no doubt that Britain, and particularly East Anglia, as America's forward nuclear base would be first to be targeted. There was no other way the Soviet Union could strike back against the US. It lacked both aircraft carriers and bombers of sufficient range to make a direct attack on North America, but Soviet bombers were perfectly capable of reaching Britain.

The situation was also crystal clear to the American Government. The safety of the US depended on American nuclear capacity in East Anglia. The USAF Secretary, Thomas K. Finletter, sent a revealing top secret memorandum to the US Secretary for Defense on 7 July 1950. He wrote:

> We are dependent at this moment almost entirely on the availability of UK bases for the launching of our strategic countermeasures. I haven't any real doubt that the British will come along if we do get engaged in war. But the question is when. I do not like at all the fact that we are almost entirely dependent on the UK ... I know the British well enough to know that sometimes they can be very slow; and this strategic countermeasure is something we cannot afford to be held up while the British Cabinet is debating about things.[8]

The other side of the coin was expressed in the same year by the British Chief of Air Staff: 'The present situation,' he wrote, 'whereby the United States could launch atomic bomb attacks on Russia making use of United Kingdom bases and facilities (without consultation) is intolerable.'[9]

These chapters tell a large part of the story of Cold War East Anglia. Had a nuclear world war broken out, it would have been the population of East Anglia who would have been among the first in the firing line. This seemed terrifyingly likely during events like the blockade of Berlin; the erection of the Berlin Wall; Khrushchev's deployment of Soviet missiles to Cuba; and in the 1980s when, in answer to the USSR basing SS-20 missiles in Eastern Europe, American Cruise missiles were stationed in the UK.

What would have happened to the civilian population, and the contingency planning to determine how those who survived could have been governed had it ended in nuclear conflict, is an important part of the Cold War East Anglia story. The *Government War Book* provided for Regional Commissioners who were equipped with draconian powers to rule their shattered fiefdoms after a nuclear strike; even though it is clear that government experts concluded that the survival of the nation state, given the scale of death and devastation, would be questionable. In fact, the British Medical Association estimated that 33 million people would be killed in a Soviet nuclear attack.

One hundred and ten small subterranean bunkers, scattered across East Anglia and staffed by volunteers from the Royal Observer Corps, would be feeding data to the UK Monitoring and Warning Organisation and would have triggered public warnings of where the mushroom clouds erupted. Their job would have been to record the power of the explosions and track the path of radioactive fallout across East Anglia, hoping to prepare any who had survived to face the horrors of the 'nuclear winter' that would follow.

A nuclear world war is unimaginable but, as the scientists and civil servants whose job it was to plan for it knew, so too was its aftermath. How effective such a warning and recording system would have been under nuclear attack is a matter for conjecture. Truly, in an area like East Anglia, where prime targets were multiple, the survivors would probably have envied the dead. But the UK Government, in planning for nuclear conflict, had to envisage life after the bomb, even though East Anglia's strategic importance was so obvious that the prospect of large parts of the region surviving could never have been considered high.

Throughout the Cold War, UK governments agonised over a central question that had particular relevance in East Anglia – what measure of influence or control could the UK government exercise over an American president determined to use American military bases in the UK from which to launch a nuclear attack? To what extent did the formal understandings between the American and British Governments give the UK a veto on American action launched from British territory?

From the American side there was an insistence on 'loose understandings' to avoid placing any limitation on a president's 'freedom of action'. Successive British prime ministers, not unnaturally, sought a guarantee that they would have a voice or a veto in any nuclear attack decisions mounted from British territory. Whether there was ever a 'cast-iron' resolution to this crucial question is open to doubt.

The agreements, such as they were, stem from December 1950, and talks between Clement Attlee and President Harry Truman.[10] Three American B-29 bomber groups had moved into East Anglian bases at Marham, Lakenheath and Sculthorpe in June 1948. Truman told the British PM that he would not use British bases to launch a nuclear attack without consulting London, unless the United States itself was under attack. When Attlee asked for that to be put in writing, Truman refused, declaring 'if a man's word wasn't any good, it wasn't made any better by writing it down'. The British pushed for language spelling out that consultation was to be included in the official communiqué. Truman and his top advisers refused. They agreed only to a statement saying that the United States 'intended' to keep the British Government 'informed' of any developments affecting use of their UK-based nuclear weapons.

By 1950, American strike aircraft were based at seven UK bases, including those in East Anglia. After further talks the Americans agreed that British ministers could refer to a 'joint decision' when explaining this very sensitive policy to the House of Commons, but still refused to define exactly what those words meant.

A communiqué prepared for talks between Churchill and Truman, when Churchill became prime minister in October 1951, confirmed: 'the use of these bases in an emergency would be a matter for joint decision by His Majesty's Government and the United States Government'. But the Americans insisted on qualifying this by the phrase 'in the light of the circumstances prevailing at the time'. The communiqué stated that consultation would take place 'if British bases were used and time permitted'.[11] The language contained a clear escape clause, and Washington continued to reject British proposals to reaffirm the personal commitment that Truman had made to Attlee.

The issue assumed significant relevance to East Anglia after Harold Macmillan became prime minister. At the Bermuda Conference in March 1957, agreement was reached between Macmillan and President Eisenhower for the deployment to the UK of American Thor IRBM nuclear-tipped missiles. East Anglia was the location of the first complex of launch bases.

Thor required two keys to be inserted to fire it. One, the 'war/peace key', armed the nuclear warhead and was always in the possession of an American officer. The other, which activated the launch process, was held by an RAF launch controller. The rationale was that Thor could only be launched by agreement between the two governments and on the instructions of both the president and the prime minister.

When the Soviets gained a head start in the race to develop long-range rockets, with the launch of Sputnik in October 1957, the possibility of a 'bolt from the blue' pre-emptive nuclear missile strike became a greater threat than ever. Macmillan wanted to ensure clarity about the 'decision to launch nuclear retaliation'. The outcome of talks was the Murphy-Dean Agreement of June 1958. The agreement was set out in a classified document entitled 'Procedures for the Committing to the Attack of Nuclear Retaliatory Forces in the United Kingdom'.[12] The document, only released in 1997 in a heavily redacted form by the US Government, enshrined the understanding about 'circumstances at the time'. It spelled out the process of decision-making that would take place under two different scenarios – a longer-term warning of attack, labelled 'strategic', and a short warning of imminent attack, labelled 'tactical'. In the latter case it authorised the US commander-in-chief of Strategic Air Command, on his own initiative, to launch nuclear armed aircraft from British bases to proceed to a specified 'hold' line without receiving 'further definite instructions'.

The process of 'joint decision' for firing the Thor rockets was far less clear: once unleashed there was no way of clawing a missile back, and Thor was peculiarly vulnerable on its launch pad to a Soviet first strike. How separate instructions from both the White House and Downing Street could have been flashed giving clear instructions to the US and UK personnel, on remote Thor launch pads in East Anglia in the inevitable chaos of an unexpected but dire threat, remains unclear and unspecified.

When, in 1983, American Cruise missiles were being deployed in the UK as part of a policy intended to match the Soviet deployment of SS-20 missiles in Eastern Europe, and public concerns in Britain were rising, the Murphy-Dean Agreement was still being referred to in secret discussions inside the UK Cabinet as the benchmark for control arrangements between the two governments. To reopen the issue, it was stated, 'would be seen as a lack of confidence in the good faith and good judgement of the US administration'.[13] Washington was deeply concerned at any suggestion that understandings over the principle of 'joint decision' should be amended to refer to 'joint control'. In US law there could be no acceptance of any dilution of the power of an American president as commander-in-chief of American forces, even if those forces were based on the sovereign territory of a foreign land.

An extraordinary paragraph in the Cabinet papers released in 2013 suggested: 'In the unlikely event that in a crisis the President appeared unwilling to fulfil his obligation to consult the UK Government it would in the last resort be possible for British personnel at the base to be ordered to take action which would make it virtually impossible for the Americans to launch their weapons.'[14]

However, the Cabinet papers on specific nuclear release procedures for the Cruise missiles, and the 'understandings' between the US and UK Governments on their use and the UK bases that housed them, which became the target of sustained protests by the Greenham Common women's camp, still remain secret, retained in classified Cabinet Office files.[15]

Those who remember the 1940s, the Battle of Britain and the threat of invasion, recall what seemed at the time to be the 'miracle' of deliverance.

The Cold War, and its ending a quarter of a century ago in the wake of the dramatic fall of the Berlin Wall, and without the horror of nuclear conflict, ought to be looked upon as an even greater deliverance. But in the twenty-first century, unfortunately, we still live in a world from which the spectre of nuclear threat is by no means lifted. That is the Cold War legacy.

According to the Ministry of Defence, the number of nuclear weapons that remained across the globe in 2013 was well over 17,000.[16] The Cold War years imposed a chilling threat and, for those who lived through them, the insecurity has never quite gone away. Despite the ever-present chill that nuclear war could be just around the corner, the Cold War did imply a kind of stability. Today's world, in contrast, is terrifyingly uncertain.

NOTES

1 Hansard, 15 February 1951.
2 Public Records Office (PRO), DEFE 10/402. 'Note on the Concept and Definitions of Breakdown', 10 June 1960.
3 Sir Kevin Tebbit, 'British Security Policy from Cold War through Peace Dividend to Force for Good in the World; A Personal Experience', first Peter Nailor Memorial Lecture, Gresham College, 2001.
4 Bermuda Conference, March 1957.
5 The National Archives (TNA), CAB 134/1476. 'Form and Duration of a Future War', 19 March 1958.
6 Catterall, Peter (ed.), *The Macmillan Diaries II*, entry for 4 November 1962.
7 Schlosser, Eric, *Command and Control* (London: Allen Lane, 2013), p. 75.
8 USAF Secretary Thomas K. Finletter. memo to US Secretary of Defense, 7 July 1950.
9 Marshal of the RAF Sir John Slessor, 1950, quoted in Campbell, Duncan, *The Unsinkable Aircraft Carrier* (London: Michael Joseph, 1984), p. 34.
10 'Use of Atomic Weapons', Attlee-Truman Agreement, Truman-Attlee Conversations, December 1950. Record Group 59, Department of State Records.
11 Memorandum of Conversation, Truman-Churchill Talks, 'A) The Strategic Air Plans and the Use of Nuclear Weapons', January 1952, National Security Archive.
12 The Murphy-Dean Agreement, 'Procedures for the Committing to the Attack of Nuclear Retaliatory Forces in the United Kingdom', 7 June 1958, Dwight D. Eisenhower Library.
13 TNA, PREM 19/979. 'Proposed basing of US ground launched missiles (GLCM) in UK', October 1982–Sept 1983.
14 *Ibid.*
15 TNA, PREM 19/980. 'Nuclear Release Procedures; Understandings between US and UK on use of Nuclear Weapons of Bases'.
16 Philip Hammond, Secretary of State for Defence, July 2013.

1

OPERATION JU-JITSU

WHY WERE RAF crews in the early 1950s flying deep into Soviet airspace from Norfolk, in American reconnaissance planes disguised with British roundels? Even RAF and American colleagues who were not in a discreet 'need to know' group were puzzled. It was some fifty-six years later that the true story of the RAF crews of the innocently named 'Special Duties Flight' was revealed. Like American colleagues who flew military reconnaissance missions over the Soviet Union, they operated under the motto 'alone, unarmed and unafraid'.

In the mid-1950s, RAF Sculthorpe, near Fakenham, was the biggest USAF base in Europe with some 10,000 personnel. It was home to the 47th Bomb Wing, equipped with the swept wing B-45 Tornado bomber with its six jet-turbine engines, part of America's tactical nuclear force. It also housed, in the pre-spy satellite days of the Cold War, a squadron of America's 19th Tactical Reconnaissance Wing, flying the reconnaissance version of the Tornado. The B-45 Tornado was the first multi-jet engine bomber in the world with the capability of being refuelled in mid-air and therefore able to undertake hazardous missions intruding way beyond the Iron Curtain. The reconnaissance version had a special pod installed in its bomb bay which contained a series of specialist cameras.

The USAF was all too aware of the problems it faced if called upon to successfully hit back at targets in the Soviet Union from its forward bases in East Anglia. Its tactic of flying at high altitude to avoid Soviet air defences, probably at night or in poor weather conditions, meant visually identifying its strategic targets would be far from accurate. It could not rely on navigation beacons to direct its bombers since the signals emitted could not be transmitted far enough into Soviet territory. It urgently needed some form of detailed mapping. Radar images of its specific targets offered a solution. Radar footprints of towns, airfields, and geographical features presented an easily identifiable image. But the bomb aimers needed actual photographs of the radar images to work from. These could only be obtained through hazardous reconnaissance overflights deep within Soviet territory.

The charismatic and notoriously 'gung-ho' head of Strategic Air Command, General Curtis LeMay, urged President Harry Truman to authorise overflights so a series of necessary radar images could be built up. Truman refused to give his permission. Worse, he placed a presidential ban on reconnaissance missions into Soviet airspace, worried that discovery would provoke the USSR into war. It was not in LeMay's nature to accept opposition, even by Presidential authority. Under the cover of operations in the Korean War, his crews managed to photograph some targets in the eastern islands of the Soviet Union. But that left un-surveyed the far more significant targets in the populous and industrial areas of the western half of the USSR which would need to be attacked by bombers operating out of East Anglia.

LeMay knew the mapping of these critically significant targets was essential to his command's mission. He made the point forcibly to his immediate superior General Nathan L. Twining and the other American chiefs of staff. Their response was to consult their UK allies. Would the British carry out this hazardous reconnaissance and share the information gained?

The British chiefs of staff were keen to build on the close relations developing between the RAF and Strategic Air Command, but in Westminster the politicians and particularly Prime Minister Clement Attlee were hesitant. However, when Churchill was re-elected a few months later, he immediately gave his consent – it was the kind of challenge that appealed to him. The deal agreed was that the USAF would provide the aircraft and the RAF would fly the missions. The radar maps produced would be shared between the two.

Records of the Air Force Historical Research Agency[1] show that on 4 August 1951 three RAF crews, led by Squadron Leader John Crampton DFC AFC, reported to Barksdale Air Force Base in Louisiana to take part in a training programme with crews of the 91st Strategic Reconnaissance Wing. Crampton had taken over command from a veteran of the famous Dambuster raid, Squadron Leader Micky Martin, who had failed the rigorous medical tests the Americans deemed necessary for flying at high altitude. Crampton had an exemplary Second World War record behind him, having flown Halifax aircraft for Bomber Command 1943–45 and Meteors and Vampires with Fighter Command post-war.

Colleagues picked for the covert group included Flt Sgts Joe Acklam and Bob Anstee from the RAF's 115 Squadron, Flt Lt Bill Lindsay and Sgt John Hill from 35 Squadron, and Flt Lt Rex Sanders who was on a staff appointment at the Air Ministry. The true reason for the unconventional training posting was known only to two of them: Crampton and Sanders. The others thought they were assessing the RB-45C reconnaissance aircraft for possible future RAF use.

After a brief introduction into American methods of strategic reconnaissance, the RAF party moved on to Langley Air Force Base in Virginia for 120 hours on training operations. By 2 September, the three crews had successfully completed that course and moved on to Lockbourne Air Force Base in Ohio for intensive flying experience on the Tornado. Ground instruction on a raft of widely different subjects followed, including the effects of high-altitude flying on the human body, the mental hazards to be overcome and the theory and operation of the pressure-demand oxygen system American crews used. Radar, radarscope target photography and the techniques of air-refuelling were among other essentials the RAF men mastered. Each of the three RAF crews was brought up to combat readiness and required to fly repeated simulated combat missions.

The RAF group returned to Sculthorpe in early December. There, as mixed RAF/USAF crews, they underwent further intensive training. USAF records reveal that, in early 1952, a directive was received at Sculthorpe from the headquarters of the Seventh Air Division to transfer four RB-45C aircraft to the Royal Air Force.[2] Three would be needed for the secret operations. The fourth was held in readiness as a spare. Out of sight in one of the hangars at Sculthorpe, two of the aircraft were stripped of all USAF markings and repainted, replacing the United States stars with the red, white and blue roundels of the RAF. The other two aircraft were flown to nearby RAF West Raynham, where another hangar was cleared for a group of mystified UK airmen to strip and repaint them.

Sqn Ldr Crampton formally took command of what was now christened the RAF's 'Special Duties Flight'. Questions were asked by those not privy to the secret operations, but cover stories were provided on the lines that the RAF unit was being trained in mid-air refuelling techniques, a manoeuvre not part of RAF flying training at that time. Meanwhile, the RAF crews were busy familiarising themselves with the APQ-24 radar camera, working closely with the RAF's Photographic Reconnaissance Unit at RAF Upwood.

In March 1952, Lt Col Marion 'Hack' Mixson was despatched from the States to Sculthorpe to take charge of the Strategic Air Command detachment to which the RAF's 'Special Duties Flight' was attached.[3] On 21 March, the first RAF special mission was flown by a single RB-45C Tornado crewed by Crampton, Sanders and Sgt Joe Acklam as co-pilot. Taking off from Norfolk, they flew to Germany where – as a test of Soviet reaction – they flew a provocative course up and down the sensitive airspace of the Berlin corridor, flying at speed and at maximum altitude.

The following month, on 16 April, Crampton and Saunders were summoned to Bomber Command Headquarters at High Wycombe for a restricted briefing on the real mission. There they saw for the first time what was expected of them. Plotted on a large wall map were three routes into Warsaw Pact territory. The first was from Sculthorpe to the Soviet Baltic States. The second tracked through Germany towards Moscow and Belorussia. The third went further south, plunging towards the centre of Russia and then arcing south to cross prime industrial complexes in Ukraine.

By giving approval to the spy flights, Churchill knew he was taking a huge political risk. The House of Commons at the time was divided in its attitude to the USSR, especially as Russia had proved a vital ally against Hitler's Nazi Reich during the war. Many prominent Labour politicians were still sympathetic to the UK's wartime ally. Churchill risked an outcry that could have resulted in his downfall as prime minister if the overflights resulted in one of the RAF-liveried American planes being brought down in Soviet airspace. But Churchill understood the crucial need for the potential intelligence and he believed it to outweigh what could have led to a highly explosive international scandal; one that might even have triggered war.

Returning to Sculthorpe, Crampton and Sanders briefed their companions in the 'Special Duties Flight' on the potentially dangerous missions they were facing. Flt Sgt Bob Anstee had survived fifty bombing trips over Germany in the war. He did not fancy pushing his luck further. His response was, why us? Why have we been lumbered with this hazardous task?

Years later, Anstee recalled that the flight plans and the targets they were expected to photograph were mostly in heavily protected areas south of Moscow.[4] In case they were shot down and captured, the crews were given cover stories. They were to convince the Soviet authorities they had got lost as a result of a navigational error or equipment failure. They carried false navigation plots and maps to back up that story. Anstee said he felt it would have been difficult to make the cover story stand up if their aircraft was recovered and the Soviet military saw all the advanced navigational equipment it carried.

Crampton's comments were just as pithy:

In the event of one of our aeroplanes falling into Russian hands, the United States would point to the paint job and disclaim all knowledge. Similarly the RAF would state that it had no RB-45C's in its inventory. How well this improbable tale, told by a 6ft 6in old-Harrovian would go down with the Russians was fortunately never put to the test. Our story would be that we were lost, a gross professional insult to my crew and myself, but an acceptable one if the dire need arose – and we would have false charts to back up our claim.[5]

On 17 April, three RB-45C aircraft sporting British markings were wheeled out of the hangars at Sculthorpe. Rumours quickly spread around the base. It was the first time most of the American personnel had seen USAF aircraft painted in RAF colours. Some time after leaving Sculthorpe the RAF crews joined up with their USAF tankers. Two were refuelled over Denmark and the third over Germany. Having topped up their tanks, all three planes switched off their lights and turned into the blackness of the night, headed for Soviet airspace.

Bob Anstee:

Once we left Copenhagen on our way in there were quite a few lights and ground features you could see from the air. Lights on the ground always give you some reference but once you get into Russia itself, Russia is one large black hole with lights, odd lights here and there. Nothing like flying over a densely populated country or flying over any big areas like France and Germany. So therefore when you do see lights they really stand out and the way we went in there was very little. There were big areas we were supposed to be photographing, most of them armed installations that were not lit. Once we came up south of Moscow itself you can see all the lights. Moscow is a big place and lit up so you do get a good reference point from that.[6]

Asked about his thoughts when he saw Moscow stretched out below, Anstee commented: 'I thought I would be very happy when I didn't see it any longer and was going the other way.'

The southerly route, which was also the longest, was taken by Crampton and Sanders. It meant they had to fly about 1,000 miles into unfriendly territory before they could set course back out again. On the way home it was necessary to take on further fuel, making the total flying time of the mission some ten and a half hours. Crampton recalled that his most abiding memory of the trip was the apparent wilderness they were flying over – it was so quiet as to be distinctly eerie.

When all three aircraft had returned to Sculthorpe the film was rushed to the RAF's Central Reconnaissance Establishment (CRE). Soviet airbases and Soviet air defences featured high among the targets they had successfully identified and the radar footprints they had brought back. This was, of course, crucial information in the event of war. In the 1950s nuclear conflict seemed highly likely. It was the really dangerous period of the early Cold War years. Had war broken out, America's Strategic Air Command would have needed to strike swiftly and accurately at the USSR's bomber bases to prevent the Soviets eliminating targets in the UK, chiefly East Anglia, which housed the American nuclear forces in a pre-emptive blow.

The Soviet military had detected the intruders but had been unable to stop them. This was an embarrassment that led to a military commission being convened in the USSR to discover what had gone wrong and to reassess the effectiveness of Russian air defences and their ability to detect and bring down any further similar missions. The results from the American point of view had been so valuable that Crampton and Sanders were asked to return to Lockbourne Air Force Base, Ohio, on 6 May for General LeMay to congratulate them in person. LeMay was known for his gruff no-nonsense manner, but face to face with him in his office the two RAF officers were treated generously and courteously, praised and rewarded with an offer of being transported and hosted wherever they wanted to go at USAF expense. They chose to spend a couple of weeks in Washington before returning to Sculthorpe and back to their units.

The Americans had recognised the success of the operation and so too had the British. Less than four months later, Sir John Slessor, Chief of Air Staff, was writing to General Vandenberg in the States proposing a follow up venture to be conducted under the codename 'Operation Ju-Jitsu'.

In October 1952, Sqn Ldr Crampton received orders to reassemble his 'Special Duties Flight' and prepare for another sortie into Soviet airspace. Some of the group's original members were no longer available. Bill Lindsay for one had been injured in an air crash. The two new recruits were Flt Lt H. Currell and Flt Lt McAlister Furze. Training occupied the next five weeks and then, without warning, the operation was suddenly called off, presumably for political reasons.

Fourteen months passed before there was a further summons to congregate at Sculthorpe where another month of refresher training took place alongside American crews. The RAF men were introduced to new, improved radar and cameras with the expectation of obtaining even more impressive results should the politicians give the go-head to another intrusion over Soviet territory. As before, Rex Sanders was summoned to Bomber Command Headquarters to learn that again three routes had been allocated on very similar courses to the first mission. One was to the north of the USSR, one over-flew the centre of the country and the third tracked across areas to the south. In each case the intention was to penetrate deeper over hostile territory in search of more strategic targets.

This was to be a much more co-ordinated effort. The crews were told that GCHQ's 'Y' Service, the wireless intercept arm of intelligence, would monitor the whole operation in order to glean as much as possible about how the Soviet Air Force and Soviet air defences were organised and how they would react. As well as GCHQ monitoring, aircraft flying close to the Soviet border would eavesdrop on the Russian response. 'Everything was extremely secret, very few people in the Air Force knew about this. Very few in Bomber Command. We were sworn to secrecy. I never even told my wife about it,' Sanders recalled.

The aircraft, again sporting RAF roundels, were wheeled out of their hangars at Sculthorpe on the evening of 28 April 1954. Sqn Ldr Crampton was again taking the longest and most difficult southern route. It required him to fly more than 1,000 miles across the Soviet Union and to collect radar images of some thirty targets, concentrating mostly on bases of the Soviet long-range bomber fleet.

He recalls that the crews were ordered to maintain complete R/T silence unless attacked, in which case they were allocated an OMG ('Oh My God') frequency only for use in a desperate emergency. Again, the aircraft left North Norfolk and flew towards north Denmark to rendezvous for their top-up refuelling.

Sanders recalled: 'We were zigzagging from one target to another in a piece of evasive routing which, I suppose, might have added to our safety. I don't know. It certainly prolonged our time over Russia.'

Like the previous mission it was an extraordinary gamble. Unlike last time, however, this sortie stirred up a hornet's nest of hostile activity. The whole Soviet Air Defence system went to major alert. The commander of air defence in the Kiev region, General Vladimir Abramov, looking back on that night nearly forty years later, described how he had ordered his pilots to try to ram Crampton and Sanders' aircraft.[7] 'Since it was the dead of night and at that time our MiGs carried no on-board radar, we tried to direct pilot Batyshev and another pilot into a head-on collision,' he recalled. The other pilot, Lt Nikolai Sysoev, remembered: 'Ideally we weren't meant to ram head-on, but to ram the most vulnerable parts of the plane.' Soviet ground control was guiding the MiG pilots but in the darkness they failed to find the intruder. However, for Crampton and his crew there were other, more obvious problems, as he explained in an article entitled 'Russian Photo-Shoot' published in *Air Pictorial* in 1997[8] after the classification of the spy missions had been lifted:

> My reverie was rudely interrupted by the sudden heart-stopping appearance of a veritable flare path of exploding golden anti-aircraft fire. There was no doubt about it; it was very well predicted flak – dead ahead and at the same height as we were. My reaction was instinctive – throttles wide open and haul the aircraft round on its starboard wing tip until the gyro compass pointed west. I began a gentle 100ft per minute descent because that made us seem to go a bit faster, although it didn't because we started juddering in the limited Mach number buffet. So I eased the power off a bit, but kept up the descent on the 'it seems faster' principle and since we had been predicted I thought it best to change height as well as speed and direction and thus giving the gunners down below three new problems. Poor old Rex piped up, 'Hey, what about my photos?' I replied succinctly, explained that clearly we have been tracked very accurately, told him about the flak burst and requested a course to steer to Furstenfeldbruck, our refuelling rendezvous and declared alternative in an emergency. We had about 1,000 miles to go and I urged Mac to keep his eyes peeled for fighters which might pick us up outside the flak pattern. Much later, I learned that there were fighters about with orders to ram us. Maximum speed was essential. I flew the aircraft just on the right side of the buffet, it sort of trembled affectionately. I had time to reflect that the earlier flashes we had seen below us had been ground fire and that our stately progress, as ordered by Rex, had given even the dimmest battery commanders time to track us and fire. The earlier attempts had all misjudged our height and thank God the Kiev defences had misjudged our speed; they had chucked everything up a few hundred yards ahead of us.

Crampton said that he thought momentarily of jettisoning the now empty 1,200-gallon wing-tip tanks to add a few more knots to their speed. But he quickly decided against it:

> Once found, their maker's name and address would have revealed that they came from America and there would have been the devil of a row. Anyway, the

thought of them bouncing down the High Street of Kiev west at two o'clock in the morning disturbing the ladies and frightening the children did not appeal. We were not flying over Russia to do that! Moreover, General LeMay would not have been best pleased at my scattering extensive bits of his aircraft over Russia. So, we kept the tanks on and finally, after what seemed an eternity, met up with our tankers but, for the first time, the refuelling boom refused to stay in our aircraft. Fearing our refuelling system had been damaged over Kiev, I thought it wiser to land at Furstenfeldbruck and refuel in the conventional way. This we did and then flew home without further incident. It was good to see the other two aircraft back at Sculthorpe and to hear that their crews had successful incident-free flights.

Crampton added:

The story would not be complete without a tribute to those who set up the whole exercise, in particular General LeMay, who was determined to get the best target information for his aircrews, and Winston Churchill, who agreed the RAF's partici- pation. A tribute must also be paid to Mr Llewellyn who, at the time, was Bomber Command's chief scientific officer and played a practical hands-on role improv- ing the quality of our radar pictures and even giving them a stereoscopic effect. Finally, I still wonder how the Russians knew where we were.[9]

In 2009, just a year before Sqn Ldr Crampton died, he wrote, in a letter to an acquaintance: 'Let it be clearly understood from the start – we survived by pure luck.'[10] He added that the RAF crews were told very little of the back- ground to the operation. 'Why were we attached to an elite USAF RB-45C Strategic Reconnaissance Squadron? Why didn't the Yanks fly the missions? It was only at the end when I realised that when you do not tell the Squadron Leader and his aircrew they cannot tell the Russians in the unlikely event of their surviving a successful shoot-down.'
Crampton continued:

In early 1951 the Russians were fed up with American recce aircraft flying over their territory and so Khrushchev told Harry Truman that Russia would consider it an act of war if America sent one more recce aircraft over his country. This put the wind up the American President who sent for General Curtis LeMay, C-in-C Strategic Air Command, and told him no more recce aircraft over Russia … LeMay went immediately to the Pentagon and called for a meeting with the Joint Chiefs of Staff. He told them it was essential that the target information was obtained. The Russian nuclear targets had to be destroyed in the first ten minutes of World War III, not just the first day. Since the President had banned him from sending any more recce aircraft out, would the Joint Chiefs get on to Westminster and ask if the RAF would do the job if necessary in the USAF's RB-45C's? Attlee, the PM, did not like it at all but his intelligence blokes persuaded him to at least form an RAF Special Duty Flight only to go out with his permission if all was clear. So Attlee agreed. The Vice Chief of Air Staff asked Squadron Leader Micky Martin, the last surviving Dam Buster pilot, to form the flight, but Micky failed his explosive decompression test so it was back to the day job and someone else had to be called. Get Crampton, perhaps the only operational type in Bomber Command at that time with jet experience.[11]

Crampton added a PS to his letter, pointing out that perhaps it was fortunate Churchill was back in Downing Street when the two 'ops' were flown in '52 and '54!

Flt Lt Rex Sanders was later asked what he thought of Churchill's gamble.[12] He replied that he was in no doubt Churchill had personally approved the operation. 'It was an amazing decision and very much reflects the character of Churchill. It was a great risk. Had we gone down there would have been quite a furore.' He was asked: 'Was there a risk of the Soviets mistaking the missions as nuclear attacks?' 'It did cross our minds that they might be thinking that we were doing something more serious than just taking reconnaissance photographs. We had no real way of knowing what they would make of it. It did cross our minds that they might think this was an actual attack by three aircraft.'

In 1992, the Soviet armed forces magazine Red Star carried an article by the Russian military writer Lt Col Anatoli Dokuhaev about the Ju-Jitsu flight. He acknowledged that the air defence units involved perceived the flights were for reconnaissance purposes rather than a nuclear attack but they could not rule out the possibility that the intruders had nuclear weapons on board. The air defence network recognised the aircraft as American and thought there were being flown by American crews.

It was the last sortie of its kind undertaken by the RAF in American planes. Russian air defences were improving, and the speed and altitude the RB-45 flew at operationally was considered inadequate to risk any further attempts at running the gauntlet of the Soviet's improved technologies.

It was many years before files recording these Sculthorpe missions flown by the RAF were declassified, but records of another daring RAF operation which provided both the Americans and the British with vital information on

Russia's emerging missile programme are still not available in the National Records Office at Kew. The official UK Government position for years was that the mission never took place. However, confirmation of the daring daylight operation flown in August 1953 emerged in *At the Abyss: An Insider's History of the Cold War*, a book written by a former Secretary of the USAF, Thomas C. Reed, and published in 2004.[13] According to him, and he was undoubtedly in a position to know the true facts, it was this flight to the Soviet secret rocket testing range at Kapustin Yar, and the vital information it brought back, that rang warning bells in Washington over the progress of Soviet rocket scientists, prompting President Eisenhower to energise America's own rocket and missile programme and eventually resulting in East Anglia becoming the launch-pad for the West's first operational nuclear missiles. There was growing concern in Washington at the time that America had fallen behind in the armaments race and the Russians had opened up a 'missile gap' that threatened America's safety.

Another American publication also provides proof that the operation which involved Cambridgeshire-based crews did take place. R. Cargill Hall, historian for the United States' National Reconnaissance Office, published a paper in the late 1990s, in the *US Military History Quarterly*, entitled 'The Truth About Overflights'.[14] In it he gave a detailed account of the Kapustin Yar mission, and confirmed that it had indeed been carried out by an RAF Canberra. The aircraft had been specially prepared by being stripped of all excess weight and with additional fuel tanks fitted in its bomb bay. It carried a special camera with a 100in lens. Reports of a new Soviet missile testing site near the Volga River to the north of the Caspian Sea, east of what was then called Stalingrad, reached Western intelligence in early 1953. The Kapustin Yar site was being referred to as possibly the most important military missile testing range in the USSR. German scientists who had been working on the V-2 programme during the Second World War had been captured by the Russians, and had been assisting with a major Russian rocket programme. American and British authorities were insistent that the test site must be photographed, whatever the risks.

America's U-2 spy plane was still being developed, and the US was in need of an aircraft which would be able to undertake the dangerous operation. In the UK, the Canberra had just entered RAF as a jet-engine bomber. In the United States, Richard Bissell, senior CIA officer responsible for planning reconnaissance flights over the Soviet Union, asked his top scientific adviser, Richard S. Leghom, to research high-altitude aircraft that could assist the Americans to photograph crucial targets. Leghom was convinced the Canberra could fill the role, providing it was suitably modified.

Experts from English Electric, the Canberra's designers, were invited to the US. They suggested its performance could be boosted by fitting more powerful Rolls-Royce Avon 109 engines to three of the aircraft on their production line – WH726, WJ573 and WJ574. The modifications so impressed the CIA that the Americans approached the British Government to ask if the RAF would be prepared to put the superior range, speed and altitude of the Canberra to use on the hazardous mission of a daylight photo reconnaissance overflight of Kapustin Yar. Churchill again gave his permission, although he had serious reservations about the possible consequences should the operation go wrong. The significance of this mission can hardly be exaggerated.

The Canberras which undertook the operation were almost certainly from 540 Squadron, a Canberra specialist reconnaissance unit based at RAF Wyton in Cambridgeshire. Evidence points to the main aircraft being the specially adapted Canberra WJ574. RAF Wyton was at that time the RAF's centre for signals and intelligence-gathering flights along the periphery of Soviet airspace. On this occasion, however, to give the aircrew more range, and perhaps to emphasise American involvement, the Canberra was first flown from Cambridgeshire to West Germany. It began its mission from Giebelstadt, a US base located 8 miles south-east of the city of Wurzburg.

The evidence is sketchy, since documentary proof from British Government papers, if indeed they still exist, remains withheld. But it would appear from 540 Squadron records that, on 27 and 28 August 1953, 'long range operational sorties' were flown by Wg Cdr Freddie Ball, Sqn Ldr Don Kenyon and Sgt Jim Brown in WH726, accompanied by Flt Lt Garside, Flt Lt Shield and Flt Sgt Wigglesworth in a second Canberra, WJ574. On 28 August, Flt Lt Shield was replaced by a colleague: Flt Lt Reeve. It is probable that one of these sorties, most likely that on 28 August, was the Kapustin Yar overflight. The use of two aircraft was normal procedure on operational missions. If the lead aircraft experienced technical problems, a spare was immediately available to take the main role. Otherwise, the accompanying aircraft acted as an observer to ensure no telltale contrails were being left which might alert the Soviet defences. Both aircraft had three crew members on board. Normally the Canberra was flown by a crew of two. The importance of the 27 and 28 August flights is clear from the fact that both aircraft carried the additional crewman to cross-check the accuracy of the navigation and to operate the camera.

Squadron records indicate both aircraft left Giebelstadt at about 1 a.m. on 28 August, flying under cover of darkness. This would have enabled the lead aircraft to arrive over Kapustin Yar just after sunrise.

There is evidence to suggest WH726 was fitted with a new highly sensitive camera, equipped with a 100in focal length lens developed by the brilliant US camera expert, Jim Baker. Just two months before the Kapustin Yar overflight, there had been an approach from the US Secretary of State for Defence to the British Chief of Air Staff for an agreement in principle that the new camera could be tried out on a Canberra.

Taking off from Giebelstadt, the Canberras headed east, climbing to 46,000–48,000ft. Warsaw Pact forces tracked them along their route over Czechoslovakia, Poland and Ukraine. Attempts were made to intercept the intruders but flying at extreme altitude the Canberras were too high for the MiG pilots. Some Soviet pilots tried to use a technique of zoom-climbing, then rapidly firing off a canon burst before stalling and losing height. As the lead RAF plane approached its target, one MiG pilot did manage to achieve a few hits on the Canberra. The aircraft was not seriously damaged, but bullet holes in its airframe caused a slight vibration which resulted in some of the camera shots of the rocket range being partly blurred. Nevertheless, sufficient clear photographs were taken before the Canberra's crew turned south-east over the Caspian Sea and headed for an airfield at Tabriz in Iran, the closest friendly base to the Russian border.

After the end of the Cold War, Lt Mihail Shulga recalled trying to intercept an RAF Canberra in the Kapustin Yar area:

> I began to climb to 48,000 or 48,500ft and ground control said, 'Look around you'. I looked up and there a few thousand feet above me I saw the plane. They asked me, 'Can you see it?' I said yes, I can: it's shimmering beautifully in the sunshine. They said: 'Prepare your guns'. So I accelerated and climbed up towards the plane – 4,000ft, 5,000ft, 5,500ft higher and my plane was stalling. Nothing came of it. The plane was flying higher than me. They said: 'Do it again'. I tried again. 'Can't you reach it?' 'No, I can't.'[15]

According to Thomas C. Reed, the former Secretary of the USAF, another Russian witness to attempts to down the Canberra was a former Soviet Air Defence radar operator who, in 1960, defected to the West. He recalled the confusion that had surrounded attempts to intercept the British aircraft. In one area the air defence operator sent fighters west instead of east, in another the Soviet interceptors ended up firing at each other in the confusion. The whole episode and the failure of the Soviet air defences led to a major enquiry and many high-ranking Soviet officers were removed, purged or sent to punishment battalions.

Reed's comment on the venture, and its impact on America's military surge to get a ballistic missile programme up and running, was generous: 'If not for a few brave British fliers, the missile gap might really have come to pass', he wrote. 'Russia might well have stolen a genuine advantage rather than the false lead in missile technology that Khrushchev boasted of when he claimed, with typical bluster, that the USSR was turning nuclear tipped missiles out "like sausages".'[16]

The Kapustin Yar mission provoked the Russians into overhauling and improving their air-defence system. Daylight overflights were considered increasingly hazardous until the Americans developed an aircraft able to reach an even higher altitude – the U-2. The first U-2 sorties over Eastern Europe took place in June 1956, but even that aircraft was not immune from being brought down, as subsequent events would show.

Meanwhile, the RAF Wyton crews were called upon to mount a number of other photographic 'spy' sorties throughout 1954 and 1955, under the code name 'Operation Robin'. These involved using an F-22 'Bomb Camera' which captured images looking out of a window cut in the port side of the bomb bay of the same Canberra aircraft that led the Kapustin Yar flight, WH726.

The aim was to fly at 40,000ft, travelling parallel with the East German border for a distance of around 40 nautical miles while photographing targets deep inside Warsaw Pact territory. The range of the F-22 camera was impressive. When it was being put through operational trials over the Channel it was found to be capable of snatching clear photographs of St Paul's Cathedral in central London.

When Harold Macmillan became prime minister he reached an agreement with President Eisenhower to allow the use of American airbases in East Anglia for U-2 spy flights. These missions, flown under the veil of the closest secrecy, took place mainly from Mildenhall in Suffolk and Alconbury, in Cambridgeshire. But there was also occasional British participation.

In mid-October 1959, a U-2 flown by a British pilot flew out of the Watton RAF base in Norfolk devoid of any identification marks.[17] But as the Americans were to find out with the shooting down in 1960 of a U-2 (piloted by Gary Powers) over the Soviet Union, even an aircraft flying at 70,000ft was not safe from the reach of ground to air missiles. The Russians' 1960 success caused an international incident and the Paris Arms Control Conference was cancelled before it had even begun.

Other 'snooping' missions in the late 1950s and the 1960s were flown by Canberras based at RAF Watton, gathering ELINT (electronic intelligence) using sophisticated eavesdropping equipment to listen in to Russian transmissions.

The Soviet authorities were well aware the UK and in particular airfields in East Anglia were being used as bases for aerial espionage. On 1 July 1960, an American RB-47 reconnaissance aircraft took off from Brize Norton in Oxfordshire. It never returned, having been tracked by Soviet fighters and shot down over Soviet territorial waters. The Kremlin sent a strong warning to the British Government about the dangerous consequences of allowing 'provocative' missions to be mounted from UK bases. The inference was that the Soviets would, in future, treat them as 'an act of war'.

The Americans denied their aircraft had been flying over Russian waters when it was chased and shot down, but the incident sparked a dispute in Parliament, and raised questions as to whether the Attlee and Churchill agreements with President Truman on the use of American bases in the UK covered covert spy flights by Americans from UK soil – and, indeed, whether the Americans had even notified the British authorities of what they were doing. Macmillan's answer was unspecific: 'The questions have a bearing on either the scope of intelligence activities, or the way in which they are conducted and controlled. It has never been the practice to discuss such matters in the House, and I have come to the conclusion that it would be contrary to the public interest to depart from precedent on this occasion.'[18]

Former US Secretary of the Air Force, Thomas C. Reed, was more open. Writing in 2004, he said of the British and American aerial reconnaissance missions: 'The aerial overflights of the Soviet Union had no justification in international law. They were espionage, pure and simple. If intercepted and shot down, those crews were dead ducks. But a handful of interesting and courageous men flew them anyway, to snap fleeting photos of the unwilling, then to head for the border.'[19]

Nearly thirty years after the 'Special Duties Flight' missions, the Americans substantially stepped up spy flights from East Anglia. The Strategic Air Command's 17th Reconnaissance Wing was deployed to RAF Alconbury in 1983 with an updated version of the U-2, designated the TR-1. Major works were undertaken at the Cambridgeshire airbase to provide hardened protection shelters for the aircraft. These served two functions: they protected the fragile aircraft, with its remarkable 103ft wingspan, from the worst of the British weather; and more importantly they masked the aircraft from Soviet observation satellites. Later, a massive hardened bunker was built in which to service electronic components of the TR-1s, and to process and analyse the reconnaissance and intelligence data captured on flights over USSR and Warsaw Pact territory. This strange-looking building was topped with a concrete 'burster cap' designed to absorb the impact of a missile before it penetrated the bunker's roof. The structure had a drive-through roadway, and extensive decontamination facilities for use in the event of radiation from a nuclear attack or from chemical or germ warfare.

Also in the 1980s, as part of the intensive spy flight programme, America's Strategic Air Command was operating SR-71A Blackbird 'stealth' aircraft, able to operate at extremely high altitude, up to 16 miles above the earth, and at speeds of 35 miles a minute, or three times the speed of sound. These were deployed from their home base in California to RAF Mildenhall in Suffolk. Two shelters were built at Mildenhall to give these very special aircraft necessary protection. A KC-135Q tanker aircraft joined the Blackbirds at Mildenhall to extend the range of their surveillance flights from the East Anglian base.

Blackbirds were equipped to provide detailed reconnaissance over an unbelievably wide area. They could photograph some 259,000km^2 of territory every hour. Most of the Blackbird espionage missions from East Anglia were for the purpose of monitoring Soviet and Warsaw Pact military deployments. Many were directed at an area of Soviet naval activity off the northern coast of the USSR, but one momentous long-range flight from Mildenhall, which required no fewer than six mid-air refuelling rendezvous, overflew the Horn of Africa, to assess Soviet military activities in that remote region.

Espionage flights from East Anglia, though never routine, became a regular feature of US operations as the Cold War progressed, but details of their missions and of specific operations remain largely hidden beneath the veil of secrecy under which units flying their highly specialised aircraft operated.

NOTES

1   USAF Historical Research Agency, Maxwell Air Force Base, Montgomery AL. Report, September 1951, of 91st Strategic Reconnaissance Wing, Lockbourne AFB.
2   USAF Historical Research Agency, supplement to May 1952 report of 91st Strategic Reconnaissance Wing.
3   http://data-freeway.com/plesetsk/overflights.htm. 'Military Reconnaissance Missions Over Soviet Union'.
4   Ross DFC, Wg Cdr A.E. (ed.), *Through Eyes of Blue* (Shrewsbury: Air Life Publishing Ltd, 2002), pp. 250–62.
5   www.spyflight.co.uk.
6   *Ibid.*
7   Reed, Thomas C., *At the Abyss: An Insider's History of the Cold War* (New York: Random House, 2004), pp. 40–43.

8 *Air Pictorial*, August 1997.

9 *Ibid.*

10 Professional Pilots Network, June 2009. www.pprune.org.

11 *Ibid.*

12 www.spyflight.co.uk.

13 Reed, *At the Abyss*, pp. 40–43.

14 Hall, R. Cargill, 'The Truth about Overflights', *US Military History Quarterly* (1997).

15 www.spyflight.co.uk.

16 Reed, *At the Abyss*, p. 43.

17 Bowyer, Michael J.F., *Force for Freedom: The USAF in the UK since 1946* (Yeovil: Patrick Stephens, 1994).

18 *The Times*, 13 July 1960.

19 Reed, *At the Abyss*, p. 47.

2

ALDERMASTON-BY-THE-SEA

THE DECISION FOR the UK to develop its own nuclear weapons was made in secret by senior members of Attlee's Labour Cabinet in January 1947[1], but the post-war Labour prime minister had set out his uncompromising view in the summer of 1945, shortly after the end of the Second World War. 'We recognise, or some of us did before this war,' he said, 'that bombing would only be answered by counter-bombing. We were right. Berlin and Magdeburg were the answer to London and Coventry. The answer to an atomic bomb on London is an atomic bomb on another great city.'[2]

Britain had made a significant contribution to the Manhattan Project, resulting in the development of the two atomic bombs which, in 1945, ended the war with Japan. The US/UK atomic partnership operated in the latter stages of the Second World War under the codename 'Tube Alloys', but at the beginning of 1946 it was becoming clear that co-operation on further research and development of nuclear weapons was likely to be brought to a close. The issue that finally ended it was the passing of the US McMahon Act, which made it a criminal offence subject to the gravest penalties, including death, to transmit any restricted nuclear information to another country. It left Britain dangerously exposed, as a mood of isolationism, followed by the Communist witch-hunt paranoia inspired by McCarthyism, swept the United States.

In Britain, fear of both American and Soviet intentions led to the Attlee government's decision. It was a further five years before the first successful test of a UK nuclear weapon. Meanwhile, crucial development work on

Britain's nuclear arsenal was taking place at Orford Ness on the Suffolk coast, the Atomic Weapons Research Establishment's (AWRE), 'Aldermaston-by-the-Sea'.

Even before development work for Britain's own nuclear bomb was put in the hands of Dr William Penny, who had been a leading partner in the wartime UK/US Manhattan Project, East Anglia was being prepared as a launch site for nuclear war: not by the RAF, but by America's newly formed Strategic Air Command. In the summer of 1946, the commander of the USAF, General Carl Spaatz, visited England to obtain permission for the use of British bases from which to mount atomic bomb missions in an emergency. He obtained agreement from the chief of staff of the RAF, Air Chief Marshal Lord Tedder, for five UK bases to be made available for American B-29 bombers. It was a secret administrative agreement struck between military officials, with no public discussion and no political debate regarding its potential implications for British sovereignty and political control. Three of those bases were in East Anglia: Lakenheath and Mildenhall in Suffolk, and Marham in Norfolk.

Shortly after the agreement was concluded, assembly buildings and loading pits for the first generation of cumbersome American atomic bombs were installed. In June 1947, the first tours to the UK by Strategic Air Command bombers began, as part of the command's mobility plan to enable America's strike force to operate from European forward bases. A year later, the American ambassador in London asked the British Government if three groups of heavy bombers could be allowed to come to Britain as a temporary 'show of strength' when Berlin became the focus of international attention, after a Soviet blockade of all land routes into the city. The 'Berlin Airlift' became the city's lifeline.

US heavy bombers on British bases appeared to be a short-term measure, but the Americans had long-term intentions. Access to British bases was critical to the Strategic Air Command's rapidly developing plans for possible nuclear war. As the US Secretary of Defense, James Forrestal, wrote at the time: 'We have the opportunity of sending these planes, and once sent, they would become somewhat of an accepted fixture.'[3] The Americans had every intention that his observation would become true. Three bomb groups arrived at Marham in Norfolk, and Waddington and Scampton in Lincolnshire, for 'operational training'. They were due to stay for thirty days, but that period was extended to sixty days and, when the first tranche of aeroplanes left, they were replaced by other groups. A process of regular 'rotation' followed and became routine. As the US Secretary of Defense had predicted, the arrangement became permanent and accepted.

This was followed by the development of the largest USAF base in Europe, at Sculthorpe in Norfolk. In 1952, just as the UK was demonstrating the successful test of its own nuclear bomb, Sculthorpe became the home of the 47th Bombardment Wing and the 20th Fighter-Bomber Wing, which provided tactical nuclear weapons support to the Supreme Allied Commander Europe (SACEUR). By 1957, 10,000 American personnel were based there. East Anglia was now a prime target for the USSR, and it would remain so throughout the Cold War as America's nuclear strike forces were deployed in the region and Britain's nuclear deterrent forces also increasingly looked to East Anglia for bases.

Churchill was well aware of the threat when he warned the House of Commons in February 1951: 'We must not forget that by creating the American atomic base in East Anglia, we have made ourselves the target, and perhaps the bull's eye of a Soviet attack.'[4]

Three years later, in July 1954, Churchill involved his full Cabinet in the decision to develop a British hydrogen bomb. The great wartime leader was appalled at the prospect of a nuclear world war. Following Stalin's death, he wanted to call a summit in London in August 1954. He was worried by the argument that he knew was present in the minds of many Americans, which he summarised as:

We alone have, for the next two or perhaps three years, a sure and overwhelming superiority in attack, and a substantive measure of immunity in defence. Merely to dawdle means potential equality of ruin. Ought we not for the immediate safety of our own American people and the incidental rescue of the Free World to bring matters to a head by a 'show down' leading to an ultimatum accompanied by an Alert?[5]

At the time, the British chiefs of staff were expressing real concern at 'the danger the United States might succumb to the temptation of precipitating a forestalling war' even if it risked massive devastation to Great Britain, since Russia was 'most unlikely to provoke war deliberately during the next few years when the United States will be comparatively immune from Russian attack'.

The Atomic Weapons Research Establishment (AWRE) at Aldermaston was where the research, development and manufacture of all elements of Britain's nuclear bomb took place, but there were issues around the design of nuclear weapons which required extensive testing. This was where the remote and secret offshoot of Aldermaston, located at Orford Ness on the Suffolk coast, came in. Through two world wars, Orford Ness had been a defence experimental station specialising in bomb ballistics. Its expertise extended back to the days of the Royal Flying Corps in the First World War. Now, in the Cold War, for sixteen years from 1954, Orford Ness played a major role developing the UK's nuclear arsenal, both the atomic and the H-bomb. Sophisticated experiments undertaken there on successive versions of Britain's nuclear armoury entailed a wide range of ballistic and environmental safety tests.

As part of the AWRE, 1,200 acres of coastal Suffolk became a top secret site vital to perfecting the UK's first nuclear deterrent. For personnel working there, the sinister implications of the work they undertook was partly shielded by the jocular name they used to refer to prototypes of the potentially deadly bombs they were handling. They called them 'cans of tomatoes'!

Orford Ness' research had two primary purposes. The first was to carry out ballistic tests on a variety of nuclear bomb casings to prove which could be dropped accurately from around 40,000ft, and whether their trajectory accorded with their design properties. Combined with this was the testing of complex trigger mechanisms built into different versions of Britain's prototype nuclear bombs to ensure elaborate firing relays would work as planned, at the right height and with the correct timing, under operational conditions. These trigger devices could only be proven by dropping the bombs and then monitoring the results. The radioactive cores of the weapons were replaced by dummy cores of similar weight and dimensions. However, the bombs still contained the considerable quantities of conventional explosive, in some cases up to 2.5 tons, necessary to initiate the nuclear explosion, so caution had to be taken or a disaster could occur.

The trials had to be flown in clear weather because the weapons' trajectory needed to be followed visually and accurately tracked. The first ballistic test, of a 'Blue Danube' bomb – the first nuclear weapon in the UK arsenal – was undertaken on the Orford Ness range on 6 July 1955. The bomb was dropped from a height of 12,000ft, from a Valiant flown from RAF Wittering in Cambridgeshire, which was then Bomber Command's Armaments School. Later that month the first successful trial to test the internal workings of the bomb took place.

Blue Danube's ballistic properties were found to work almost too well. When released the bomb tended to gain lift and 'fly' nose up below the tail of the Valiant, virtually bumping along the aircraft's body. To cure this, strakes were fitted to the underside of the fuselage forward of the bomb bay to disturb the airflow and give the bomb an initial push downwards.[6] Blue Danube was a large weapon, and experimental drops were made with modifications in shape to achieve ultimate performance and the required trajectory in flight.

In September, further trials took place to test the effects of dropping Blue Danube from different altitudes and at different speeds. Some fifty air drops were made over Orford Ness during the Blue Danube series of ballistic tests. Activity at Orford Ness was stepped up in anticipation of Operation Buffalo, the atomic bomb live trials at Maralinga in South Australia where, over the course of a number of weeks, two nuclear devices were exploded on steel towers, a third on the ground, and a fourth dropped from a Valiant. This last was the first viable nuclear weapon dropped from the air by the RAF.

The Orford Ness experiments included a range of stress tests which subjected the bombs to every conceivable situation they might experience under operational conditions: for instance, the vibrations involved when the bomb was being transported or loaded into the bomb bay of an aircraft; the movements and stresses of flight; extremes of temperature and humidity, and the stresses of speed and deceleration. Each needed to be accurately simulated and inflicted on the dummy nuclear weapons, without fear of them either causing a premature triggering of their complex firing mechanisms, or damaging delicate and sensitive control features.

The first nuclear bombs were equipped with a variety of trigger devices to control when, and how, they would explode. These components were less sophisticated than those installed in later weapons. Nevertheless, some of the electronic equipment developed for Britain's first nuclear weapons represented significant technical developments.

The Blue Danube series of bombs required regular maintenance and servicing to keep them in operational readiness. Radar switches could detect their height above the ground so that the bomb could be triggered at a predetermined height to maximise the effects of an airburst; or they could be activated at a set height by barometric switches which provided back-up if the radar trigger failed or was subject to enemy jamming. Mechanical timed and impact fuses, powered by battery or a turbo generator, were also incorporated in the bombs. So, too, were flip-out fins which were opened by compressed air after the weapon left the bomb bay.

Each of these needed rigorous testing, under real flying conditions and in widely different environments, to ensure they would operate as planned and not malfunction, even when robustly handled. The safety of armourers, aircrew and the public depended on these exacting tests. In operational use these weapons would be stored on bases close to public areas, so there was a paramount need to be certain that they were totally safe from possible unintentional detonation. Safety was the overriding responsibility of the scientists working at Orford Ness.

'Blue Danube', the name given to the UK's first nuclear bomb, referred not just to one weapon but a series of closely related variants, the product of continuous improvement and modification. Blue Danube was a colossal weapon: it weighed 10,000lb, was 24ft long and had a diameter of 5ft. Its nominal yield was 15 kilotons. Though cumbersome, it was aerodynamically very stable and its qualities as a freefall bomb were largely down to the rigorous ballistic testing on the Suffolk range.

The first Blue Danube weapons were delivered to RAF Wittering, Cambridgeshire, in November 1953. Wittering was the Bomber Command Armament School (BCAS). Prior to 1953, the RAF had had no experience in dealing with nuclear weapons, so the BCAS was staffed by RAF personnel who had assisted in the design and development of nuclear weapons at Aldermaston. The station's operations record book hailed their delivery as 'marking a historic month for this unit, and indeed for the Royal Air Force and the country. During this month the first atomic bombs have been delivered to the RAF, and they are now held by this unit. These bombs will raise the striking power of Bomber Command to an order completely transcending its power hitherto.'[7]

Variants of the initial Blue Danube, some of which delivered a yield as high as 40 kilotons, were available for operational use until the early 1960s. Blue Danube was then succeeded by upgraded weapons given equally exotic codenames. Most underwent similar ballistic and environmental tests at Aldermaston's Orford Ness offshoot.

'Red Beard' was a relatively lightweight tactical fission bomb, using a tritium-boosted plutonium/U235 composite core. Much smaller than its predecessor, it measured 12ft long and about 3ft in diameter. 'Violet Club' was an interim air-dropped bomb with a hugely boosted yield, estimated at 500 kilotons. It was very much an experimental stopgap weapon to get the UK into the thermonuclear age. Alarmingly, it was inherently unstable.

Violet Club was first delivered to RAF Wittering in February 1958. The government sanctioned its delivery for operational use to prove, at the first possible date, the UK's thermonuclear capacity. Although its development programme was incomplete, it now appears that corners were cut and it was deployed with some severe strictures, despite concerns expressed by the controller of armaments at the Ministry of Supply. In their book, Planning Armageddon, Stephen Twigge and Len Scott assert that, at the time of its deployment, the operational effectiveness and safety of the weapon was in some doubt.[8] 'As Violet Club took a minimum of thirty minutes to prepare it could not be placed on quick readiness alert unless safety measures were relaxed. Once the safety device was extracted from the weapon, it immediately became live.' The warhead contained enough uranium 235 to form an uncompressed critical mass, so it was feared that if a mechanical deformation occurred, a small explosion or an accident in which the weapon was dropped could result in a full yield nuclear explosion. The fact that five of these weapons were assembled on Bomber Command stations across East Anglia over the following months raises the question, how much safety was compromised and what level of risk was the region subjected to?

Violet Club was followed by Britain's first true H-bomb, codenamed 'Yellow Sun', which had a yield in the megaton range. The initial tests for the first British H-bomb were within the Blue Danube shell, but the final operational version of the weapon had a different design, with a blunt nose to induce a high drag-factor to slow down its rate of fall to enable the delivery aircraft to turn away and escape the massive blast.

To accommodate all the necessary tests to be carried out on the developing British nuclear arsenal, a series of unique concrete and shingle test chambers were built at Orford Ness. At its height the base had five test laboratories, and the remains of some still exist. The most impressive were constructed in the early 1960s to carry out a test programme on the series of nuclear bombs generically known as the 'WE177'. These weapons had an explosive mechanism based on the American W47 system.

Technically, it presented a serious problem. The conventional explosive in the core of the bomb was liable to explode prematurely if the weapon suffered a heavy accidental blow. Rigorous testing to improve its safety was therefore crucial. A set of substantial buildings, known as 'pagodas', were designed to absorb the blast from an accidental detonation. They had robust walls shored up on the outside by shingle abutments, and enormous roofs supported on pillars that had substantial wide overhangs. Between the roof and the walls were gaps to allow the blast to vent and therefore limit any damage.

The theory, thoroughly tested on small-scale models before the buildings were erected, was that debris would be directed downwards onto the shingle by the overhangs. The roofs of these structures consisted of 3ft of concrete topped by a 7ft thick layer of shingle – a material of which there was a plentiful supply at Orford Ness. Had an explosion occurred, the roof would have lifted and then fallen back, burying the test chamber beneath and so diminishing the spread of debris and any nuclear radiation. Although the nuclear cores were missing from the bombs tested at Orford Ness, some nuclear material remained which could have caused a limited radiation risk.

Within these pagoda-like test laboratories, and those built earlier for the first generation of nuclear bombs, complex equipment was installed: electronic vibration machines, powerful centrifuges for studying the effect of 'G' forces on bomb components, and instrumentation to reproduce extreme climatic conditions and atmospheric pressures. The climate tests subjected the weapons to variations in temperature ranging from 60°C to −60°C. The simplest, but possibly most hazardous tests were carried out in a 'drop zone' unit, where a bomb could be hoisted and then physically dropped onto a concrete floor, simulating a possible bomb bay failure resulting in a nuclear bomb being accidentally deposited onto a concrete runway – an incident that happened several times on operational bases in East Anglia.

The experiments were thorough. The drop tests were backed up by further experiments involving propelling a weapon along a 25-yard rocket-sled track. This was to simulate dropping a nuclear bomb by parachute and allowing it to skid along the ground before detonation, enabling the delivery aircraft to safely make its escape. The weapon was secured to the sledge, the rocket ignited and the bomb fired at 150mph headlong into a concrete wall. The object was to check that the delayed action trigger mechanisms would work as planned – at least ten seconds after impact.

While all these tests were essential and hazardous, the most spectacular were those flown on the ballistics range, where test bombs were dropped into the sea to satisfy the scientists that the various internal trigger mechanisms worked accurately. Details about the operation of these mechanisms were communicated, by telemetry, to the control centre where the results were recorded and analysed. The orange-painted bomb was tracked and filmed as it fell into the sea with a spectacular splash some 400 yards offshore. In an early bombing trial the splash was so eye-catching that someone reported it as the crash of a light aircraft and the Aldeburgh lifeboat was launched to go to the scene.

Initially bombing runs were flown at 40,000ft but, as Soviet air defences improved, tactics moved in favour of low-level attacks. This form of low-altitude tactic was exhaustively tested at the Orford Ness range. An aircraft would approach fast and low in a shallow dive to 500ft, then climb away rapidly, releasing the bomb as it pulled up so that the weapon was lobbed in a trajectory towards its target and allowing the aircraft to escape from the ensuing nuclear blast.

As Britain's nuclear deterrent switched from its V-bomber force to submarines, a special facility was built at Orford Ness designed to test the warhead of the Polaris ballistic missile. Security at Orford Ness, while it functioned as a satellite of the AWRE at Aldermaston, was strict. Its geographic location and remoteness, cut off from the mainland by a tidal creek, contributed to its secrecy. Entry was closely controlled. Scientists and engineers worked under a regime of 'need to know' and steps were taken to ensure that there were never any references to atomic weapons research. No identification that could lead people to associate the site with nuclear bomb testing was allowed.

Personnel were told that, if they were asked whom they worked for, they should give a non-committal reply along the lines of 'employed by the ministry'. They were told always to be on their guard, and never to get involved in conversations that might be overheard on the mainland, particularly in local pubs. But, whatever those living in the locality thought might be taking place at Orford Ness, the Russians were in no doubt. Russian spy trawlers, furnished with copious arrays of eavesdropping aerials, were often seen lurking off the Suffolk coast. They frequently moored up in Hollesley Bay to monitor what was going on, and listen in to whatever radio traffic they could. When the Russians were seen in the area, radio traffic and some test procedures were suspended. Ironically, one or more of the Russian spy trawlers were from a fleet of twenty which had been built in the mid to late 1950s at the Brooke Marine shipyard, a short distance down the coast at Lowestoft, supposedly for the Russian fishery authorities!

One group of tests was carried out with particularly heightened secrecy. They were on nuclear explosive charges that were being developed to demolish every tactically important bridge – road, rail or river – in West Germany, should a Soviet invasion be launched and it were to become necessary for NATO to mount a desperate bid to prevent the Russians sweeping across Germany and beyond. A detachment of the SAS was detailed to escort these highly secret weapons to Orford Ness, and back to Aldermaston where they had been developed.

The last Aldermaston test took place at Orford Ness in June 1971. The gates of AWRE Orford Ness were finally closed after sixteen years of nuclear weapons development, in October that year.

NOTES

1   TNA, PRO, CAB 130/16, GEN 163/1st Meeting 8 January 1947. 'Confidential Annexe Minute 1. Research into Atomic Weapons'.

2   TNA, PRO, CAB 130/3, GEN 75, Papers 1945–47; GEN 75/1 'The Atomic Bomb', memorandum by the prime minister, 28 August 1945.

3   US Defense Secretary James Forrestal, diary note, 17 July 1948.

4   Hansard, 15 February 1951.

5   TNA, PREM 11/669. Draft Cabinet paper on 'Two-Power Meeting with Soviet Government'.

6   Wynn, Humphrey, *RAF Nuclear Deterrent Forces* (London: HMSO, 1994), p. 96; John Allen, former senior scientific officer at Farnborough, 'Suffolk and the Bomb', Radio Castle, November 2013.

7   RAF Wittering operations record book, November 1953.

8   Twigge, Stephen and Len Scott, *Planning Armageddon: Britain, the United States and the Command of Western Nuclear Forces 1945–1964* (Amsterdam: Harwood Academic Publishers, 2000).

3

THE NUCLEAR PENTAGON

IN THE LATE 1950s and early 1960s many East Anglian towns were frighteningly vulnerable to a Soviet first strike. Few were potentially more at risk than Thetford. It was sited uncomfortably close to multiple strategic targets. Had the heat been turned up on the Cold War, and it was an alarming possibility at the time of the Cuban Missile Crisis in 1962, the historic town of Thetford would not have been a comfortable place to be.

Two of the UK's largest USAF bases, at Mildenhall and Lakenheath, lay 10 miles away in one direction, while 8 miles in another was a front-line V-bomber base, RAF Honington. Nuclear weapons were stored at all three. Feltwell, the RAF's first nuclear ballistic missile base, and the launch site of three Thor missiles tipped with nuclear warheads, was just as close. Another four missile bases, where a further twelve Thor rockets were deployed, lay within a radius of 13–20 miles. These were Tuddenham, North Pickenham, Shepherd's Grove and Mepal. Marham, another operational V-bomber station, was around the same distance away.

All were assumed to be prime Soviet targets, but closest and most secret of all, 2 miles down the road just across the Norfolk border in Suffolk, was one of only two storage and maintenance depots for Britain's first generation of nuclear bombs. RAF Barnham covered 23 acres, and had storage igloos for fifty-seven fissile cores for the 10,000lb Blue Danube bomb, the first purely British nuclear weapon issued to the RAF. It also had comprehensive facilities for the maintenance of the complex technical components and conventional explosive elements which comprised the bomb's internal mechanism.

Barnham was built, cloaked by the Official Secrets Act, under the aegis of a secretive government group called the 'HEROD Committee', a body charged with introducing the atomic bomb into service with the RAF. The name 'HEROD' was designed to be intentionally obscure, but to those in the know it spelt out the words 'High Explosives Research Operational Distribution'. Its job was to advance plans for the storage of the UK's nuclear bombs and the design of the buildings required to maintain them, and to ensure the extremely high level of security surrounding the project. HEROD was the architect of Barnham and its sister 'Special Storage' site at Faldingworth in Lincolnshire. HEROD's other task was to provide the trained personnel needed to handle the nuclear weapons, from their delivery to the RAF through to their despatch on operational missions. HEROD was also responsible for planning the nuclear weapons training school based at the Bomber Command Armament School (BCAS) at Wittering in Cambridgeshire.[1] Since the RAF, at that time, had no experience of dealing operationally with atomic weapons it was decided to staff the BCAS with RAF personnel who had worked on the design and development of atomic weapons at the Atomic Weapons Research Establishment at Aldermaston.

An internal government report on 27 August 1953 stated that Barnham should be ready for use by 1 May 1954, and the first training course should start at Wittering in January the same year.[2] Meanwhile, the report said that facilities for two-bomb storage 'clutches' at four operational airfields at Marham, Honington, Wittering and Waddington should be ready by early 1954. The first two Blue Danube bombs were actually delivered to Wittering in November 1953 and, until the special storage bases in Norfolk and Lincolnshire were ready, Wittering was the only base capable of holding the RAF's first generation nuclear weapons.

Security at Barnham from the day it opened was substantial. The entire nuclear development programme was shrouded in secrecy, and knowledge of it limited strictly to those people actually involved. Indeed, it was as a result of the atomic weapons programme that PV (positive vetting) security procedures were introduced.[3] Former personnel who underwent the 'deep' security vetting found that not only were their own past contacts checked, but those of their families and friends as well.

Known to the personnel working there simply as 'Top Site', Barnham was hidden from the nearest road by heathland and shrub. A paradise for wildlife and birds, the surrounding land was dotted with gorse bushes or, as one former Barnham serviceman called the spikey unforgiving plant, 'nature's own barbed wire'! It was impregnable to any without the highest security clearance.

The inner site, where bombs were stored and worked on, was surrounded by security fences topped by triple strands of barbed wire. A 7ft-high concrete wall shielded what went on within the 'sanitised' central area from prying eyes. Electric gates, seventy floodlights, prowling police dogs, armed guards, trip wires and 27ft high watchtowers equipped with powerful searchlights ensured that no one without the correct security clearance gained entry.

It was so highly secure that its true purpose never leaked. Rumours abounded, though. One myth spread locally was that it was a breeding centre for monkeys to be used in a non-existent British space programme. As one officer stationed there recalled: 'Outside the wire we simply didn't talk about our work.' Casual observers were discouraged, or if they persisted, challenged. Drivers of vehicles stopping for any length of time on the Barnham–Elveden road, leading to the A11, one of East Anglia's main arteries, found that they were rapidly accosted by armed service police and, at night, picked out in the beam of powerful searchlights.

I was living in Thetford during some of the Cold War's most dangerous days. To have known what was stored there would have severely increased the fears we all felt in those worrying days at the end of October 1962, as Khrushchev's attempt to confront America with missiles he had covertly slipped into Cuba threatened to bring nuclear conflict, which inevitably would have drawn in Europe as well.

One former officer at the base, then a Flight Lieutenant, now a retired Air Commodore, recalls:

> The surrounding heath was kept under close surveillance by sharp-eyed RAF police, equipped with powerful binoculars up in the 'goony towers', as one or two of us who took our girlfriends exploring in the area soon discovered! Everyone who worked there was required to sign the Official Secrets Act and be vetted for reliability. Those with direct access to the weapons and their nuclear cores were vetted to a much higher level, and a few to one of the highest levels then existing. We adopted a generally low profile.[4]

Another former Flight Lieutenant at Barnham remembers: 'We were all very security conscious and security-cleared to the highest level. Talking out of turn would not have occurred to us, even within our families.'[5]

David Twyford, one of the first dozen RAF police deployed to Barnham, who served at the base 1954–55, remembers: 'We were from a generation of people who, if you were told to keep quiet about our job, we kept quiet. You knew how sensitive what went on there was, but you didn't talk about it out of a sense of duty.'[6]

Barnham served as the nuclear weapons storage and maintenance facility for V-bomber stations in No. 3 Group of RAF Bomber Command located in the south of England – bases like Honington, Marham and Wittering. When the first Blue Danube atomic bombs were delivered to Wittering in November 1953, the station's operations record book noted the event had totally transformed the strike power of Bomber Command.[7]

As production of Blue Danube and its subsequent variants came on stream, each operational base in the UK was provided with what was termed a 'Supplementary Storage Area' designed to hold twelve nuclear weapons or, as they were referred to, 'SWs' (Special Weapons), and thirteen vaults for the nuclear cores. This was considered a sufficiently lethal 'clutch' for the 'first strike' element of the V-Force.

Barnham's role was to hold the reserve stocks of Blue Danube for distribution to operational stations in No. 3 Group for 'second strike' missions. It also received bombs from the operational stations for a cycle of regular maintenance and servicing. Barnham's sister nuclear storage facility at Faldingworth, near Lincoln, served V-bomber stations further north, in No. 1 Group.

Should a nuclear conflict break out, the UK's initial response would have been launched with the bombs already available on the bases. Barnham and Faldingworth would then have been responsible for providing weapons for back-up sorties. Air Commodore Mike Allisstone, then a Flight Lieutenant working as a convoy commander at Barnham, recalls 'hoping that we would be able to get these weapons forward to the front-line airfields and depart again before they became the subject of further attention by the Soviet forces, although how long I expected to survive thereafter scarcely entered my head'.[8]

Blue Danube required frequent inspection and maintenance. As bombs were rotated through Barnham for servicing, there were regular convoys carrying nuclear weapons to and from the base. Similarly, there were frequent convoys between Barnham and the Royal Ordnance Factory at Burghfield near Reading, and the Atomic Weapons Research Establishment (AWRE) at Aldermaston. Barnham's operations record book mentions fifteen to twenty armed convoys a month.[9]

Barnham was laid out in the shape of a pentagon. Most of the site, which since it was sold by the MOD in the late 1960s has flourished as an industrial estate, remains much as it was in the late 1950s and early 1960s.

Because of its national significance and historic importance, some of the buildings on the base have been listed and are being renovated to preserve them and to illustrate what went on behind the security fences in the early days of the UK becoming a nuclear power.

The high level of security is obvious to see. Steel watchtowers, equipped with powerful searchlights, guard each of the five points of the pentagon, positioned to give a clear line of sight along the surrounding fences and the wide sterile area in between. The tower at the front of the secure area overlooks an inner electric security gate. From these 'goon' towers, and from a sixth elevated viewpoint on top of a repair and maintenance building near the front of the secure compound, armed RAF police kept watch twenty-four hours a day, monitoring activity outside and inside the wire. Constant armed patrols ensured the perimeter was secure. No chances were taken. RAF policemen had to 'clock in' regularly at various points on their routine patrols around the site to get a security card time-punched and to prove that they had checked all the areas allocated to them.

From time to time the effectiveness of the security was tested by small groups of RAF security police from other units who attempted to breach the sanitised inner area. None succeeded. Two high fences, topped with barbed wire, protected the front of the base. Each had an access point with an electric security gate sliding on rails. In effect this provided a vehicle trap between them. When operational, the sterile area was floodlit by seventy lamps. RAF police with dogs patrolled inside it, and trip wires linked to flares were deployed to ensure no one could cross without alerting the armed guards. There was also a public address system installed to warn off anyone who strayed too close, and to alert personnel in the event of a hazardous situation arising. Although the precautions taken ensured that a nuclear disaster was virtually an impossibility, the nuclear weapons with their fissile cores removed still contained considerable amounts of conventional explosives. If an accident had happened, as well as causing substantial blast damage, some radioactive contamination could have resulted.

The buildings at Barnham fell broadly into four categories: those providing accommodation and facilities for the RAF police and administrative purposes sited outside the inner security walls; those used for the storage of the bombs minus their fissile cores; small kiosk-like buildings in which the nuclear cores were held; and maintenance buildings in which inspection and servicing took place.

Originally, there were three large stores for the main components of Blue Danube, located on an oval circuit road around a central area enclosed by a substantial earthen blast mound or traverse. Two of these buildings remain, and the third was burnt down in a fire in the 1980s. Each storage building is surrounded by 14ft-high blast mounds, 65ft wide at the base and bolstered by reinforced concrete walls. These precautions against a massive explosive blast were needed as Blue Danube, and its successor Red Beard, contained conventional explosives as well as fissile material – in the case of Blue Danube, as much as 2.5 tons of high explosives in each weapon.

The implosion system used in both nuclear bombs consisted of a hollow sphere into which the nuclear core was inserted when an aircraft took off on an operational strike mission. The extensive blast walls around the storage buildings were to deflect a conventional explosion upwards, and away from other nearby bombs, should an accident happen. In theory, if one of the three large storage sheds blew up, the explosion would have been contained and neither of the other two should have been affected. The buildings were designed so that any explosion internally would blow the walls outwards, leaving the building's framework standing.

To reduce any danger of sparks, the floors were treated with a specialised 'pitch mastic' finish, a form of mastic asphalt resistant to solvents, which were regularly polished and 'hoovered' with industrial cleaners to eliminate dust. Heating and air conditioning kept a stable environment which was essential for the bombs' sensitive mechanisms. Each of the three stores was provided with a gantry at its entrance, extending over the roadway and built of reinforced concrete columns and beams to facilitate components being lifted from a transporter or trolley and moved inside.

Stuart Robathan worked at Barnham 1954–59, and was responsible for the storage of nuclear bombs in one of the three storage buildings. He recalls the strict regime of cleanliness. 'A dust-free environment was essential and we had a schedule to remove any possible dust or airborne contaminants by vacuuming the centre section of the building regularly. In storage the weapon's outer skin was removed to provide adequate ventilation around the weapon's centre core.'[10] The temperature and humidity in the building were controlled to maintain a constant environment, and readings were checked frequently. Those working in the storage areas were required to wear anti-static footwear. Any visitors were asked to put on overshoes. He estimates that the store he worked in held ten to twelve bombs, each broken down into the weapon's centre, nose and tail sections. Because of the strict 'need to know' policy he had no knowledge of the number of bombs being held in the other two stores, but it is reasonable to suppose that the storage capacity of each was similar. 'Security was an extremely high priority. Personnel were only allowed access to buildings to which they had been given authority, whatever their rank.'

Derek Morris was stationed at Barnham as a storeman for six years, between late 1955 and 1961. His security clearance allowed him access to most of the storage and maintenance buildings. Like Stuart Robathan, he recalls the floors of the three main storage areas being kept spotlessly clean and highly polished. 'They were so clean you could have eaten your dinner off them,' he recalls. He confirmed that the storage buildings each contained an average of ten to twelve bombs at any one time, a total of around thirty-six on site, although some of the weapons were for training purposes. 'The live bombs were painted green with a red nose band. Those for training purposes were black with a yellow nose band.'[11] Derek lived in the billets on site.

Security was so tight, on the basis of 'need to know', that when bombs or parts of bombs were being removed from storage and loaded for convoy removal, they were screened from the view of the RAF police on the watch towers. Heavy curtains were hung inside the massive steel doors of the store sheds, and drawn across whenever the doors were opened. Security passes were colour coded, denoting which personnel were allowed to enter which buildings. Derek's own high security rating took six months of background checks in order to satisfy the authorities that he was a suitable person to be entrusted with the responsibilities that matched his clearance.

The freefall Blue Danube bomb was bulky and heavy to handle. It was 24ft long and 5ft in diameter, and weighed 10,000lbs. The earliest weapons had a nominal yield of 10–12 kilotons, but subsequent variants were developed with yields up to 40 kilotons. According to declassified papers, only some fifty-seven of an original target of 200 Blue Danube bombs were ever built.[12]

The technology of nuclear weapons moved on rapidly and by 1961 its successor, Red Beard, smaller and more easily handled, was coming on stream. Derek Morris recalls that some American nuclear bombs, smaller and more complex, were also stored at Barnham in the early 1960s, but Barnham never reached the capacity for which it was built, and developments in nuclear strategy, in storage capacity at operational V-Force bases, and later in the introduction of a stand-off bomb, made it redundant within a few years of it being opened.

Two weapons' maintenance buildings, separated by a massive blast mound 158ft by 40ft, stand opposite the main gates to the secure area. Entry to one of the buildings seems to have been via a form of air lock or security system that ensured the inner doors could not be opened until the outer ones were closed. Stuart Robathan recalls that the reason for the double doors was to ensure secrecy, to make certain that the uncovered centre core, the explosive component, of the Blue Danube bomb was not exposed to the view of any personnel without the necessary security clearance.

The second maintenance workshop was used for the servicing of the sensitive electrical and electronic components, built into the nose section of the bomb, which determined the height at which the nuclear explosion was detonated. Blue Danube had three sections – a tail unit which held parachutes and gas bottles to extend the fins; a central section which contained the explosive lenses, forming a precisely machined sphere; and the nose cone, packed with electronics and radar units. The presence of a photographic dark room suggests that X-ray equipment may have been used to detect minute cracks in the casing for the high-explosive lenses which surrounded the nuclear core.

All the doors leading into the main servicing areas were secured by combination locks. Only those with the correct clearance were allowed to see the bomb in its stripped-down state, and it is clear that the authorities went to great lengths to make sure this happened. Indeed, many of the papers relating to Blue Danube are still classified, and many question marks remain about what exactly took place in these storage and maintenance buildings.

Blue Danube worked on the implosion principle. Moving from the outside to the centre, its main components comprised thirty-two detonators triggered by an impulse from a firing device, which itself incorporated other auxiliaries like safety switches and arming circuits. Detonation had to be started simultaneously in all thirty-two lenses. The lenses were finely engineered shapes, irregular hexagons and regular pentagons, designed to fit perfectly together, containing a combination of fast and slow explosives so that transit of the firing impulse from the detonator to every point on the inner spherical surface of the lens was simultaneous.

The detonation then reached a spherical shell of homogeneous high-explosive called the 'supercharge'. Within the supercharge was a uranium tamper, which converted the convergent shockwave, reflected some of the neutrons back into the fissile material, and increased the efficiency of the explosion. Within the tamper was the plutonium, and within that the initiator. This last component was needed because, although the implosion resulted in a powerful compression of the fissile material and the surrounding tamper, the material would stay compressed only for a few microseconds and then expand again very rapidly. It was essential to make sure that the chain reaction started at exactly the right moment. This was done by creating an intense neutron source at the centre of the fissile material. The implosion compressed the uranium core into a dense supercritical mass, which triggered a chain reaction, or 'fission', and the instant release of a huge amount of heat and radiation in a nuclear explosion.

To understand and maintain Blue Danube required personnel with knowledge of physics, mathematics, chemistry, metallurgy and telemetry. It was exceedingly specialised work, and personnel, trained at the Bomber Command Armament School at Wittering, operated on a strictly 'need to know' basis. Those who worked in administrative and stock control roles at Barnham, even though they might be of superior rank, were unaware of what took place behind the walls of the maintenance and storage buildings.

Blue Danube resembled a scientific experiment on a gigantic scale, rather than a fully developed weapon. It was not engineered to be subjected to all the rigours of service life like subsequent nuclear bombs issued to the RAF. It needed regular servicing and careful monitoring to maintain its reliability and safety.

There is still much to be revealed about how exactly Barnham operated and the true purpose of all the buildings on the site. One other building stands prominently near the entrance to the highly secure area. Described as an 'inspection and repair workshop', it was not built until 1959 and, unlike the other maintenance buildings, was light and airy with tall glazed windows. It is probable that it was built to assemble weapons to an almost operational state at Barnham, following removal of most British-built weapons from RAF operational bomber bases after the introduction of more powerful American 'Project E' nuclear weapons. This resulted in British early generation nuclear bombs being taken from on-base storage units and returned to Barnham, where they were held in reserve and prepared for use in potential 'second wave' attacks.

Project E arose out of the 1958 US–UK Mutual Defence Agreement, under which American nuclear weapons were provided for use by the RAF as part of a fully integrated strike plan, codenamed 'SIOP' (Single Integrated Operational Plan). However, the nuclear bombs remained strictly under USAF control. The agreement came with 'strings' attached, as President Dwight D. Eisenhower made clear at the time: 'The US government welcomes the agreement to co-ordinate the strike plans of the United States and United Kingdom bomber forces, and to store nuclear weapons on RAF airfields under United States custody for release subject to decision by the President in an emergency.'[13]

The nuclear cores, the crucial radioactive element of each weapon, were stored separately at Barnham in small rectangular kiosk-like storage buildings, sometimes referred to as 'igloos' or 'hutches'. They were grouped in four areas, spaced uniformly off a network of concrete access paths between the bomb component stores, and protected from them by earthen blast mounds. Each had a steel-faced door, secured by a combination lock with a spring-loaded electric contact which sent a signal to a central control board in the guard room indicating whether the kiosk was open or locked. Each nuclear core storage unit was protected from the threat of a lightning strike by copper earth straps. Signs on the doors indicate that regular testing of each unit for effective protection against a lightning strike was regarded as a major safety precaution. Concrete lighting standards were sited among the igloos, each with a red panic button or fire alarm at chest height. The pathways to the igloos were lined by steel handrails, possibly to ensure personnel conveying a fissile core in its heavy steel container did not stumble and fall, or perhaps to ensure no one strayed from the walkways.

The fissile core for the bomb, made up of a composite of plutonium/uranium 235, was contained in a stainless steel vessel which fitted snugly into an aperture in the igloo floor, and was locked in place by a heavy steel lid secured by a lock. The cores needed to be checked and reassembled every few months, so there was an ongoing requirement for regular monitoring.

Air Commodore Allisstone recalls that there would always be a minimum of two people present whenever a core was moved, because of the demands imposed by the dual security system:

The site officer had responsibility for setting the combination lock on each igloo, and the underground safe inside also had a lock which I think was key-operated, the key being held by one of the weapon engineers, so there would always have to be two of us around. It would be virtually impossible, for all sorts of reasons, for anyone to make off with one of the cores. [The containers in which the cores were moved around were heavy, since they included some lead shielding, and were brightly coloured.] We never moved more than one at a time for radiation reasons, although I do not think the popular rumour that two close together might cause a chain reaction had any basis in fact whatsoever. Those who were involved in working with these cores, including carrying them, were listed by the RAF medics as 'Radiation Workers', presumably to enable statistics to be kept of the level of radiation they were subjected to. There could never have been a nuclear explosion at Barnham because the cores were only ever inserted into the weapons at airfields, and then only shortly before take-off. Even a major heath fire could not have threatened the cores at Barnham because they were underground and sealed in. But at the same time we all knew, at the back of our minds, that it was virtually certain Barnham was being targeted by the Soviets and if the balloon ever did go up we were unlikely to survive. In particular it did occur to me that the delivery to airfields of second strike weapons would have had to be undertaken under conditions where large parts of the country would already have been laid waste, and that it was therefore largely a hypothetical plan. But I never did lie awake at night worrying about that or anything else connected with the job, which was always done extremely professionally.[14]

Wing Commander Tony Howells recalled that when he was stock control officer at Barnham his main concern was the accuracy of the stock records: 'I don't ever recall being concerned with the number of items held, other than for accounting purposes.' As to the security of the nuclear cores in their storage igloos, he says: 'The Site Officer was responsible for changing the combinations and the weapons engineer had the key to the storage safe in the igloo floor.' It was a security system that would have been virtually impossible to breach.[15]

Fire was an obvious and ever-present danger, and careful planning had gone into making sure fires could be dealt with rapidly. Barnham was equipped with a fire station sited just outside the security gates, a covered above-ground water storage tank and pump house, and strategically placed static water tanks.

Derek Morris, who lived on site for nearly six years, recalls that, while there were a few trained firemen, all airmen were expected to assist if a fire ever broke out and there were regular exercises to make sure everyone knew their jobs in an emergency.

The majority of the fissile storage units have one shaft in the floor for a single core; but nine of them, grouped in threes as part of three of the arrays of nuclear core buildings, are slightly larger and contain two shafts. It is unclear whether these were for the storage of a different type of nuclear core, and why such a small proportion of the total number of igloos were constructed with double shafts. Tony Howells says: 'It has been suggested that the two-core igloos were part of a deception plan about the number of fissile cores that could be held, but there is no certainty about this.'[16] Another possibility was that the larger units were built to house cores for training bombs. As the two-core units are those closest to the inspection buildings, it has been suggested that the fissile cores might have been rotated so that the twin ones housed the next few cores either to go into or come out of the routine inspection process. However, their true purpose remains one of the unanswered questions of the Barnham site.

According to the original drawings for the igloos at Barnham, they were to have been built with an irregularly patterned roof which, from the air, would have given the impression of trees or foliage. But this refinement was dispensed with, perhaps because of the urgency of getting the site built, or more likely because the prominent shape of the site from the air would have been difficult to disguise. Another possibility is that the authorities wanted the Soviets to know that Barnham was capable of storing at least fifty-seven weapons.

A brick building, heavily shielded by brick blast walls and approached through double steel doors protected by a heavy combination lock, is thought to have been used for periodic inspections of the nuclear cores. They were considered highly unstable, and needed to be inspected regularly and reassembled every few months. Tony Howells says the cores would have been serviced at AWRE at Aldermaston, but radiation monitoring was carried out at Barnham, and it is possible this building was used for that purpose.

It seems doubtful that anywhere near a full complement of fissile cores, to fill all fifty-seven igloos, was ever held at Barnham. Air Commodore Allisstone says he has no idea why there were so many igloos:

> They probably outnumbered the storage spaces for the enormous Blue Danube weapons which were in use when I first arrived at Barnham in 1960. It is my recollection that the three storage sheds were seldom, if ever, filled to capacity but I simply cannot tell how many cores we had at any one time. It is possible that Nos 92 [Faldingworth] and 94 [Barnham] Maintenance Units were designed before the concept of holding weapons forward on V-Force airfields was developed, and at that stage it might have been envisaged that all nuclear weapons would be held at Barnham and Faldingworth until they were required for use.[17]

It is possible that some of the answers to these questions, and to many others concerning exactly what processes took place in the maintenance and inspection buildings, will never be clear until some of the secret documents about Britain's first generation of atomic bombs are declassified.

'In the early 1960s', the Air Commodore recalls:

The huge 10,000lb Blue Danube, not very different to that dropped at Nagasaki, was being replaced by the much smaller Red Beard, 12ft long and weighing 2,000lb, so we might have several Blue Danube weapons in storage pending their return to Burghfield near Reading for dismantling. At the same time we were delivering Red Beard to the front-line Supplementary Storage Areas while collecting the obsolescent Blue Danubes, and Barnham provided the necessary slack in the system to accommodate fluctuations in flow.[18]

All operations at Barnham were carried out strictly on the 'need to know' system. Mike Allisstone writes:

> Although I was privy to most of what was going on at Barnham, unless I had a valid reason I would never have attempted to enter some of the workshops where the weapons were serviced for example. I had been trained on the general principles on which they worked, not least for safety reasons, but the 'divide and rule system' ensured that if any one of us had been tempted to betray what we knew it was most unlikely our knowledge would have been sufficiently comprehensive to have been of great use to the enemy.[19]

RAF Barnham was almost a self-contained and very secure unit, although certain administrative and domestic functions were provided by nearby RAF Honington. Barnham's staff included clerks, cooks, MT (mechanical transport) drivers and weapons engineers, as well as electrical, radio and mechanical engineers. The commanding officer was a wing commander of the RAF's Equipment Branch. Squadron leaders headed up the equipment and engineering units, while flight lieutenants were responsible for each of the major sub-specialisations and were convoy commanders. Reporting to them were a number of highly trained technicians of senior non-commissioned rank and below, who had been through specialist courses in the specifics of each part of every nuclear weapon at the BCAS at RAF Wittering near Peterborough.

If the security at Barnham was so tight, what was security like when nuclear convoys went on the road, as they did regularly from the nuclear storage base? RAF Police, who accompanied convoys, were certainly armed with 9mm automatics and carried live ammunition. A typical convoy would have a couple of police on motorcycles up front, followed by a Morris J2 with the Provost Branch officer commanding the RAF police, and a couple of police corporals. Behind them would be the load carrier, a Leyland Hippo if the load was a Red Beard bomb, or a Scammell wrecker, towing a closed specialised trailer called a 'pantechnicon', if it was a Blue Danube bomb.

Sometimes convoys would consist of more than one load-carrying vehicle. Immediately following the load carrier was a safety wagon carrying fire equipment and radiation test gear. The convoy commander's J2 would come next, often carrying a couple of spare drivers, and one or two further RAF police motorcyclists would bring up the rear. The motorcycle escorts' job was to ensure that the convoy was able to get across road junctions without interruption. Should there be an accident, they would close the road in both directions and make sure that total security of the weapons was maintained.

A weapons engineer travelled in the safety wagon, and it was his job to deal with any radiation hazard or fire. The convoy commander's role was to ensure the convoy's safe transit and contain any incidents en route. He determined when and where the convoy would pull in for a break – largely pre-planned, because most laybys were too small to accommodate the whole convoy.

It was the unplanned stops that caused the problems. For instance, regulations insisted that in the event of a severe thunderstorm, to avoid the possibility of a lightning strike, the convoy should pull over and stop. Air Commodore Mike Allisstone, who often had the role of convoy commander, recalls one incident when an electric storm caught him out:

There was increasing lighting and a lot of noise, and then one exceptionally vivid flash hit a lamppost right alongside the still mobile Hippo just ahead of me, followed immediately by the loudest thunderclap I have ever encountered. The Hippo swerved into the middle of the road and stopped almost dead in its tracks – and so did the rest of the convoy. As the RAF police closed the carriageways in both directions, I leapt out of my J2 and went round to the Hippo where the driver was sitting transfixed and completely dumbstruck. We lifted him out of the cab, stiff as a board and, still in the sitting position, laid him gently as we could on the floor of my van. We then put a relief driver in his place and got the convoy moving again as quickly as possible. It transpired that our victim, having seen the flash and heard the enormous explosion just to his rear, was convinced that the load he was carrying had blown up and that he was dead! It took him several days to recover.[20]

But there were lighter moments too. Mike Allisstone recalls:

Many convoys from Barnham had to go through the middle of Maidenhead. The Hippos' exhaust pipes were fitted with spark arresters which gave out a loud banshee wail which ensured that everyone knew we were coming from that alone, notwithstanding the police escorts. These pipes were positioned so that they exhausted to the front right hand side of the vehicle, about 2ft off the ground. In Maidenhead's one-way High Street the Hippo drivers discovered that, by blipping their throttles at the right moment, they could lift the mini-skirts of the girls on the pavement beside them – so our progress through such places was both noisy and hilarious, besides doubtless being known to every Soviet agent within half a mile of our route![21]

There were hazardous incidents too. The most significant fell into a category known by the code word 'Broken Arrow', an event so serious that it had to be reported immediately to No. 10 Downing Street if there was a risk to the community at large of nuclear radiation. One such incident occurred when Air Commodore Allisstone was stock control officer at Barnham. He recalls:

One of our load carriers with a weapon in a container on board ran out of control and embedded itself in a house in Reading. The crew had used the standard procedure, for this was not an uncommon occurrence, of ratcheting up the handbrake and attempting to stall the otherwise unstoppable engine by putting it into gear and letting in the clutch. On this occasion, however, it kept running until the clutch eventually burned out amid clouds of white smoke. With the engine screaming and apparently about to explode, the occupants evacuated the cab and the driver then bravely attempted to turn off the external fuel cock. Unfortunately, before he could complete his task the vibration released the handbrake. The driverless Hippo set off down the hill, and at the first bend it encountered, embedded itself in the front room of a terraced house. Fortunately the sole elderly occupant was in the back kitchen at the time, from which she emerged dusty but unhurt, to offer everyone a cup of tea! The RAF police did a good job of keeping the local press, etc. at a safe distance and the only national publicity was a small headline in one tabloid the following day entitled 'The Secret Something in Widow's Parlour!' The 'Secret Something' was a Red Beard centre section, mounted on a wheeled frame inside a very heavy duty transit container. The nuclear core was not in place – cores were never transported in the same convoy as a weapon. However, there would have been low grade radioactive metal inside the warhead so there could have been a low risk of a radioactive leak, but fortunately in this case there was none.

We had no long range radios or mobile phones in those days and the convoy commander had to find a telephone box and sufficient small change to report the incident to me. He had to tell me, at Barnham, what had happened on an open line without giving away any secrets and having to pause every so often to put more money in the machine. Farcical by modern standards![22]

It was then Mike Allisstone's responsibility to use the direct line installed at Barnham to alert No. 10 Downing Street of the accident – the only time he remembers the hotline being used.

The heavy-duty transit container in which the weapon was secured was designed to survive an impact equivalent to being thrown off Beachy Head, so even in a serious accident there should have been little chance of damage to the weapon or indeed of nuclear contamination.

Nuclear cores were also transported to and from Barnham in armed convoys. In this case, special trailers were used in which up to three core containers could be securely anchored to the floor. Even if the vehicle overturned the cores would have been undamaged, so heavily were they protected. For good reason cores were never transported in the same convoy as a weapon!

Ron Randell worked as an MT driver at both Faldingworth and Barnham. He recalls being issued with a personal pen-meter to measure the level of radiation should a leak occur:

If the meter changed colour to yellow, that was the time to start worrying. The drivers had strict instructions that in the case of an accident they were to provide the police with only their name, rank, service number, the index number of the vehicle, say absolutely nothing about what their vehicle was carrying, and then refer the police to the Air Ministry. On one occasion in Lincolnshire another vehicle pulled out and struck the side of my Hippo when we were carrying the centre section of a Blue Danube bomb. I gave the police officer only the details I had been told I could. He seemed a bit put out when I refused to answer any other questions. But I heard no more about it.[23]

The 'Special Storage Unit' at Barnham was planned between April 1952 and the spring of 1953.[24] It became fully operational the following summer, although in the summer of 1955 substantial alterations were made to increase the security of the base. Despite the substantial cost of the base, it had a short lifespan. The ongoing development of smaller nuclear weapons, the move to thermonuclear (H-bomb) in 1961, and the introduction of the stand-off bomb (Blue Steel) in the autumn of 1962, meant that Barnham was being run down during the latter part of 1962.

No. 94 Maintenance Unit officially closed at the end of July 1963, although some RAF personnel remained at the site, presumably stripping it of any classified material, until November that year. It remained in the possession of the MOD on a care-and-maintenance basis for a couple of years more, in case there was a need for its reinstatement. In 1966 the Ministry of Defence put the bomb store up for sale. It was purchased by Mr Keith Eldred and his wife, who initially used some of the buildings to grow mushrooms on a commercial basis – an ironic twist on the destructive nuclear mushroom clouds for which Barnham was built. The base has subsequently been used as an industrial estate, but two of the three storage buildings, the igloos, the blast walls and the watchtowers and security fences have all survived, and Mr Eldred is overseeing the renovation of many of them to provide a permanent, but stark reminder of why the base was built, and the very real threat that the UK's first nuclear weapons were developed to combat.

Britain's first H-bomb, Yellow Sun Mark II, entered service in 1961. While the Mark II was in development, a small number of Yellow Sun Mark I weapons were housed at Barnham's sister site at Faldingworth for distribution to operational bases at Finningley and Cottesmore. The Atomic Weapons Research Establishment's health and safety co-ordination committee took some time to clear the weapon for operational use and, because of persistent fears over its safety, it was only authorised to be transported on roads closed to public use when the V-Force was ordered to readiness in an emergency. All Yellow Sun Mark II weapons were returned to Aldermaston by the end of 1967 to make way for the bomb that was the main thermonuclear weapon in the RAF's arsenal for the longest period of time, the WE-177, which, in successive variants, lasted until Britain's main deterrent shifted to the Royal Navy's submarine-launched Polaris missile in 1969.

At the end of the Cold War when the WE-177 was withdrawn from service, all the bombs were taken to RAF Honington, Suffolk, for storage until they could be decommissioned. By then, Honington had become the main base for the RAF Regiment, who were responsible for the nuclear stockpile's security. The last of Britain's H-bombs were finally removed from East Anglia in early 2001.

NOTES

1 TNA, 'Note on the establishment of the HEROD Committee', 10 April 1953, Director of Operations (B & Recce) to Deputy Chief of Air Staff. CMS1074/48/ DDOps (B).
2 TNA, 'Aide-memoire for ACAS (Ops) Special Weapons', CMS1074, 27 August 1953.
3 Wynn, Humphrey, *RAF Nuclear Deterrent Forces* (London: HMSO, 1994).
4 Exchange of emails with retired Air Commodore Mike Allisstone, May 2013.
5 Exchange of emails with retired Wing Commander Tony Howells, June 2013.
6 Exchange of emails with David Twyford, July 2013.
7 RAF Wittering operations record book, November 1953.
8 Air Commodore Allisstone, May 2013.
9 RAF Barnham operations record book, AIR 29/4110 & AIR 29/3274.
10 Exchange of emails with Stuart Robathan, August 2013.
11 Letter and conversation with Derek Morris, August/September 2013.
12 John Walker, British Rocketry Oral History Project, 2007.
13 Wynn, *RAF Nuclear Deterrent Forces*, pp. 258–59.
14 Air Commodore Allisstone, May 2013.
15 Wing Commander Howells, June 2013.
16 *Ibid.*
17 Air Commodore Allisstone, May 2013.
18 *Ibid.*
19 *Ibid.*
20 *RAF Historical Society Journal*, No. 26, 2001.
21 Air Commodore Allisstone, May 2013.
22 *Ibid.*
23 Interview with Ron Randell, June 2013.
24 www.airfieldinformationexchange.org, April 2013.

4

THE CALENDAR GIRL WHO MADE COLD WAR HISTORY

ROLAND HALL SPREAD the technical drawings he had made more than half a century before across the living room carpet at his home in North Walsham, north Norfolk. The yellowing drawings, in neat draughtsman's hand, form an important part of Cold War history. They represent nothing less than the blueprint for the first ever operational nuclear missile launch bases in the free world; missile bases which were one of the provocations that, along with Jupiter missiles in Turkey and Italy, persuaded Khrushchev to initiate the gamble of the Cuban Missile Crisis that took the world to the brink of nuclear conflict in October 1962.

Roland Hall's plans were the genesis of 'Project Emily', and in the coded shorthand of Cold War security, 'Emily' carried the answer to nuclear defence for the American and British governments at a time when the USSR appeared to have gained a crucial lead in nuclear rocket technology. The first fifteen of those launch pads, Roland Hall knew, would be built in East Anglia.

Why was East Anglia being catapulted into the front line of a potential ballistic missile conflict? The answer is simple. As a nation, the United States had been rocked in May 1954 when the Soviet Union successfully tested an intermediate range rocket, blasting it 630 miles down its test range, from a launch pad at Kapustin Yar. It confirmed the West's worst fears, that the Russians had the capability of using their R-5 rocket to deliver a 300 kiloton nuclear warhead over a range of about 750 miles. That put both London and Paris in its range.

In Washington, it focused minds on the need for a rapid development programme to propel the United States back into missile supremacy. President Eisenhower issued an order to develop an intermediate-range ballistic missile as quickly as possible, as a first stage on the route to building an intercontinental missile capable of striking behind the Iron Curtain from launch sites in America. Eisenhower gave the programme highest priority. He instructed the Douglas Aircraft Company to produce 120 Thor missiles, to be operationally ready by July 1959.

Developed in a remarkably short timescale for such a technically advanced project, the Thor missile stood 65ft tall and was tipped with a 1.45 megaton nuclear warhead, 100 times more lethal than the bomb that fell at Hiroshima. It had a range of between 1,500 and 1,725 miles. Once launched, the rocket had a maximum speed of 10,250mph and could reach a height of 390 miles.

While Thor was in development, the USSR delivered further shattering news. In October 1957 the USSR became the first nation to launch a man-made satellite into space. The implications of Sputnik were clear; the USSR was close to possessing the means to project a nuclear missile from behind the Iron Curtain directly onto US territory, and the Americans would be powerless to reply until they had developed their own intercontinental rocket.

There was, however, one way around the problem – base America's intermediate-range Thors in the east of England. From East Anglia, it would take Thor just eighteen minutes to hit Moscow, and US and UK military chiefs calculated Thor could reach the majority of the sixty most important targets in the Soviet Union.

The deal was agreed between President Eisenhower and Prime Minister Harold Macmillan at the 1957 Bermuda Conference, when what became 'Project Emily' was conceived.

For fifty years the origin of the project's name was shrouded in mystery, though it was the name universally used at the time on both sides of the Atlantic when referring to the construction of the first bases for nuclear missiles in the free world. Roland Hall had known the secret all along. In the late 1950s, following the historic deal in Bermuda, he and a colleague were working at the Air Ministry in London, preparing the technical plans for the launch pads, the first clusters of which would be built in Norfolk, Suffolk and Cambridgeshire. It was not an easy task. The only Thor missiles to have been launched at that time had been research and development firings from Cape Canaveral, the missile testing centre in Florida. No operational launch pads had, at that time, been constructed, or even designed. All that Roland Hall had to work on, to produce the several hundred working drawings, were details of the complex mobile units and components needed to equip a launch base, and photographs of a mock-up layout that had been created in the parking lot of the Douglas Aircraft Company at Culver City in California.

He told me: 'You may be interested in how the project received its name. I was given a Pirelli calendar with a scantily clad female on it with her name, Emily, in small print.' The lady clearly made an impression on him. 'I decided to stencil her name in large letters and pinned it on the office notice board.' The next door office was occupied by a small group of USAF representatives whose function was to administer the project in the UK in its initial stages and to sanction the work the Air Ministry was undertaking prior to the massive civil engineering task that lay ahead. 'The United States colonel came to see me one day and saw the calendar. He asked to borrow it and that is how "Project Emily" got its name.' It was also how a pin-up entered Cold War history.[1]

For communities across East Anglia the deployment of Thor raised feelings of fear and concern. The government saw the American nuclear missiles as bridging the gap until Britain developed its own 'Blue Streak' rocket. The United States regarded Thor in East Anglia as its front line base for the defence of America until its Strategic Air Command had missiles of intercontinental range.

British defence chiefs took a different view. A classified note from the British Deputy Chief of Air Staff said that basing Thor in the UK was designed to 'serve American ends more than British'. The deployment of 'these highly vulnerable missiles would make the UK a more attractive target for attack' was the bald conclusion of the British Chiefs of Staff. They regarded the deal as America's 'insurance policy'.[2] This was also the gist of a report in the *East Anglia Daily Times* in February 1959, headlined 'East Anglia is a Sitting Target'.[3] The Thor launch pads in Norfolk, Suffolk and Cambridgeshire gave the Soviets an even greater incentive to strike first and destroy them. Instead of deterring an attack, logic suggested that the Thor sites seemed to invite one.

But the die was cast, and Macmillan's government was not for backing down. Indeed, the government published a White Paper entitled, 'The Supply of Ballistic Missiles by the United States to the United Kingdom', on 21 February 1958.[4] It said that the missiles would be manned and operated by UK military personnel who would be trained in the USA at the earliest feasible date. On the control of the missiles, the White Paper said that a decision to launch would be a joint one between the two governments, but the warheads would remain in full US custody, as required by American law. This was the notorious two-key control system under which an American officer would arm the warhead and an RAF officer would use his key to initiate the fifteen-minute fuelling and launch process.

The complexities of two governments needing to agree on the command to fire Thor, without delay and under the threat of an incoming Soviet nuclear strike, were not lost on the British commanders. In February 1958 the chief of Bomber Command, Air Chief Marshal Sir Harry Broadhurst, spelt the problem out to his superior, the Deputy Chief of Air Staff:

> The V-bombers represent a relatively simple problem because having brought them to readiness, I can order them off at the first warning, but I am left with well over an hour in which to obtain a decision as to whether they should carry on and complete their attack or be recalled to base. On the other hand, as I see it, we will need two governments to agree before the IRBMs [intermediate-range ballistic missiles] can be fired but even then they could not be launched at first warning. This could only be done when the radar plots were definitely identified as hostile, or what is much more likely, after the Soviet bombs or missiles had started to fall on this country. In sum, it seems to me that given the same state of readiness i.e. fifteen minutes, whereas the V-bombers can be controlled through our present chain of command the IRBMs present an entirely different problem because the military readiness and the political decision to fire must coincide if we are to avoid having our 'deterrent' destroyed before it can be launched.[5]

The dilemma of the chief of Bomber Command was clear, and it could give little comfort to those across East Anglia living in the proximity to Thor bases which, even the top brass of the RAF acknowledged, were prime first-hit targets of the Soviet Union.

The urgent need to get the bases and the missiles operational meant pushing the project on as fast as possible, even if that meant cutting corners. As the Chief of Air Staff, Air Chief Marshal Sir Dermot Boyle, wrote in a letter to the British Minister of Defence, Duncan Sandys: 'We shall be subject to pressure from the Americans before we can be satisfied that it [Thor] has achieved a satisfactory operational performance, as evidenced by a series of successful test launches.'[6]

His concern was merited. Thor's programme of test launches in the United States did not start encouragingly. The first four ended in failure. The fifth, in the autumn of 1957, was the first to be completely successful but, while Thor had demonstrated its ability on that occasion, there were more failures to follow. Unsurprisingly, doubts about launch safety and Thor's operational efficiency remained, and Sir Dermot was echoing growing apprehension at the catastrophic consequences for the UK civilian population of an accident involving a nuclear-tipped rocket. The selection of launch locations needed to take account of such risks.

Bases down the east of England made sense; with only the initial trajectory over land to reach the North Sea the danger to the local population would be reduced, though for East Anglia risks clearly remained. Missiles fired in test launches in the States were equipped with a command destruct mechanism – explosives attached to the airframe that could be set off by remote control to blow up the missile if it flew off course. And in tests no nuclear warhead was fitted. Neither safeguard would exist on rockets based in East Anglia. Strategic Air Command refused to fit a destruct capability to operational missiles based in East Anglia for fear the Soviets might find a way to detonate them mid-flight.

The experience of Thor test launches at Johnson Island in the Pacific Ocean might have given East Anglians more cause for worry. In the summer and autumn of 1962, as sixty Thors sat on launch pads down the east coast, a series of tests took place which left much of Johnson Island contaminated by radioactive fallout. One Thor went off course and was blown up when the range safety officer triggered the command destruct mechanism. Two and a half weeks later, a Thor with a 1.4 megaton warhead shut down after fifty-nine seconds, and exploded at 30,000ft, showering the island with pieces of the missile and warhead. A month later a missile with another 1.4-megaton warhead misfired on the launch pad, resulting in a massive explosion which spread contaminated debris over the surrounding countryside together with burning fuel and radiation. Two months after that, a fourth Thor went off course ninety seconds after lift-off. Once again the island was polluted with radioactive plutonium.

Hazards weren't confined to a launch failure. Thor was fuelled with potentially hazardous liquids – liquid oxygen (LOX), which was so highly volatile that extreme precautions had to be taken to ensure a spark from static or nearby electrical sources could not set off a horrific blaze; and RP-1 kerosene, another fuel that needed to be handled with extreme caution. In July 1958, a week after the first engineers landed at Lakenheath American base in Suffolk to begin the programme of building the launch pads in East Anglia, a liquid oxygen pipe ruptured at the Douglas facility at Sacramento in Northern California and the superchilled liquid that had been frosting on the outside of the pipe instantly turned into a flaming inferno. Six men were seriously burned and three died. Perhaps it was as well that the secrecy surrounding

Project Emily kept information of this sort from the people of East Anglia, who were largely unaware of what was being deployed in their midst.

The Douglas engineers who had been sent to East Anglia to install the missile and its associated systems were ploughing a new furrow. Few had any real applied experience with the systems. As one of them, Dr Peter L. Portanova, subsequently wrote: 'A matter of weeks differentiated a seasoned veteran from someone who had only academic knowledge.'[7] He was in a position to know, having learned the hard way, as he dedicated himself to the urgent job at Feltwell, the first base to be built, and quickly earned a promotion to senior operations engineer. In this role he moved on to supervise the installation at RAF Tuddenham in Suffolk.

To impress the lessons of the LOX disaster at Sacramento, he and Douglas' chemical process engineer, Ed White, initiated a safety demonstration to illustrate the dangers of working with liquid oxygen. Using a 1ft-diameter dish, processed to be laboratory clean, he would press his thumb in the centre to introduce hydrocarbon on the dish. He then carefully poured a small amount of liquid oxygen onto the dish. From 30ft he dropped a small weight onto the dish using a string pulley. The combination of the thumbprint hydrocarbon, the liquid oxygen and the kinetic energy of the impact produced a dramatic explosion and a lesson well learned.[8]

Once work on the bases started, and certainly when the 65ft-long rockets arrived, the vulnerability of East Anglia shot up. There was no doubt that each Thor base would be a prime first-strike target for the Soviets. Prime Minister Macmillan acknowledged the fact, saying 'We can't help that, anyway' and adding that if the missiles were ever used it would mean failure of all the purposes for which they were devised – slim comfort in towns and villages in Norfolk, Suffolk and Cambridgeshire.

The Russians were alert to what was happening. A scheduled Moscow–London civilian passenger service was conveniently inaugurated in 1958, using a Tupolev TU 104 jet airliner. The routine flights regularly seemed to suffer 'poor navigation' over the North Sea. This meant the aircraft often took a flight path which passed over one or more of the missile bases. The TU 104 had, for no obvious commercial reason, a glazed nose, providing an ideal observation position from which to photograph what was happening on the ground.

The first location likely to have been placed on Russia's target list was Feltwell in Norfolk. It had been a former RAF base through two world wars, and was now destined to be Bomber Command's Strategic Missile School as well as the headquarters of the complex of launch pads that comprised the East Anglian Strategic Missile Wing. Feltwell was closely followed by

North Pickenham in Norfolk, Mepal in Cambridgeshire, and Tuddenham and Shepherd's Grove in Suffolk. Each base had three missile pads, so East Anglia provided launch facilities for fifteen missiles – a quarter of the sixty Thors to be based down the east of England – each tipped with a nuclear pay-load 100 times greater than the atomic bombs that had been dropped on Japan to end the Second World War. The locations chosen were deliberately spread far enough apart to ensure that a single Soviet nuclear weapon could not destroy all five. Little comfort for the local populations or the launch crews, since it also meant that a determined attack by the USSR would have required a number of nuclear weapons aimed at East Anglia if the threat the Thors posed to the Soviet Union was to be neutralised.

The team choosing the locations in East Anglia rejected several alterna-tives. A site at Watton was considered too close to Feltwell if the latter base was hit by a nuclear explosion; Witchford, only 2 miles from Ely Cathedral, was also ruled out because, should a missile fail to launch, the national architectural treasure might have been destroyed. Mepal was chosen instead.

British civil engineering contractors turned Roland Hall's complex drawings into launch emplacements, in a crash programme every bit as urgent as the extensive work carried out across East Anglia to build airfields to accommo-date the American heavy bombers in the Second World War. Indeed, some of the locations were on ex-wartime American bases. Each of the fifteen East Anglian launch pads was in the shape of a cruciform, built with a foundation of 6in reinforced concrete and oriented with great accuracy plus or minus half a degree of a pre-set angle to true north.

The orientation of the launch pads was crucial if the missiles were to hit their targets. The co-ordinates of the launch sites had been surveyed extremely accurately by a team from the Royal Engineers. The dominant structures of the launch emplacements were two solid 'L'-shaped blast walls to give protection to the technical trailers required for the launch process should a missile explode on the pad during the short period between engine start and lift-off. These walls were constructed from 20cm-thick concrete with a ballast infill. If a missile had been launched in anger, as no spare mis-siles were available, the pads would have been effectively redundant, but that was immaterial because they would almost certainly have been vapor-ised by an incoming Soviet warhead.

The longest arm of the cruciform formed the base, into which rails were set for the cover of the metal hangar which protected the missile when it was lying horizontal at rest. The hangar slid back automatically in the initial phase of the launch process, allowing the missile to be raised vertically on its launcher. On each side of the pad were the fuel tanks: a 6,500-gallon tank holding RP-1 kerosene and a 13,500-gallon tank for liquid oxygen. The problem of keeping the supercooled LOX at −183°C meant that the stainless steel tank was, in effect, a huge double-skinned thermos flask. Because of the high rate at which LOX was fed into the missile it had to be pressurised with nitrogen from cylinders kept on two trailers parked close to the LOX tank.

Around 1,000–1,500ft from the launch emplacement was the 'Launch Control Area', a reinforced concrete hard-standing for the launch crew's trailer, from which the launch process of all three missiles was controlled. Normally the missile lay prone in its steel shelter. The first stage in launching it was to automatically slide the shelter back on its rails and raise the missile to its full height on its transporter erector. In this position the fuelling process could begin. These first phases of launching were constantly practised on the Thor bases, the aim being to reduce to a minimum the time it took to go through all the stages of launch.

High-intensity lighting surrounded the launch pads and at night the Thor bases stood out eerily from the surrounding countryside, bathed in brilliant floodlight. An 8ft-high chain-link fence with double overhead angle bars topped with barbed wire provided security, supported by a further fence with a wide sterile zone in between which was patrolled at night by RAF police dogs. Separate from the launch pads, and behind its own security fence, was the building where the nuclear warheads known as 're-entry vehicles' were stored. This discrete area was administered exclusively by armed US personnel, out of bounds to the RAF, even to the British base commander. Alongside it was a pyrotechnic store where the igniter squibs for the missiles were kept. Both were protected by blast-proof revetments. Entry to the warhead and pyrotechnic stores was guarded round the clock by USAF police.

The contractors for the building of the East Anglia missile bases, Sir A. McAlpine & Son Ltd, faced demonstrations by supporters of the newly formed Campaign for Nuclear Disarmament (CND). The most violent clashes took place at the North Pickenham base in Norfolk, in December 1958, when nearly fifty protestors gained entry to the site, bridging barbed wire entanglements by placing placards over the sharp wire barbs and scrambling across. Some climbed onto the massive concrete mixing plant in an attempt to stop work proceeding. But they had not reckoned with the reaction of the construction workers, who grabbed many of the CND supporters and hurled them into a 6in-deep mixture of wet concrete and mud. Nor had they anticipated the action of RAF firemen who turned their hoses on them. Several protestors were treated for minor injuries. Shortly before Christmas there was a second demonstration at

North Pickenham. Forty-five demonstrators were arrested by Norfolk Police, and twenty-two, who refused to give an undertaking not to take part in further demonstrations, were held in custody over the Christmas holidays.

Through the closing months of 1958 and the early spring of 1959 tons of technical equipment were flown into the American airbase at Lakenheath to be installed at the bases across East Anglia. During the whole Project Emily programme some 6,000 tons of missiles and materiel had to be flown across the Atlantic for installation at the sixty pads that made up the Thor force in the UK.

The first chartered flight of Douglas engineers, who were to install the technical components, arrived at Lakenheath on 24 July 1958. They were followed by several hundred more whose task was to assist in bringing the UK missile bases up to operational status. Accommodating them was a problem. Hotels from Norwich to Cambridge were hired, and Lynford Hall and Brandon Park were among the country houses taken over to house them. When all other possibilities had been exhausted, trailer parks were set up.

The lack of suitable accommodation prevented all of the required American engineers from coming over to Britain. All of the housing for 50 miles around the sites was full, so 250 USAF men and a large number of RAF personnel were drafted in as 'Douglas employees'. Peter Portanova writes:

> Under the acquisition rules at the time this was not completely legal, but it was absolutely necessary to accomplish the programme. Project Emily was in the sense of the times and the fear engendered in the Cold War something that had to be accomplished whatever the obstacles. As a testament to those who participated no objections arose because the 'can do' attitude was pervasive.

The urgency of Project Emily drove the programme forward. Construction at Feltwell, the No. 1 base, started on 19 May 1958. By mid-September the first contract for pouring the concrete for Feltwell's launch pads was completed. The first missile was handed over to the RAF at Feltwell and erected into its firing position towards the end of November. The Suffolk and Cambridgeshire launch bases were completed by July 1959.

But anxiety over the operational readiness of the missiles, their reliability, and the safety of the local population remained. Up until July 1959, of the twenty-five test launches in the States only ten had been classed successful. A statement in an American TV interview made by General Bernard Schriever, the senior officer in charge of Thor development, did not inspire confidence. He said: 'We expect to have a few missiles blow up on the stand; if we didn't we wouldn't need a research and development programme.' Schriever added that the 'initial operational missiles will be about 50 per cent reliable and we are putting our first missiles overseas fully a year before we thought we could.'[9]

Thor's operational capability was not publicly acknowledged until 9 December 1959, when the Secretary of State for Air, Mr George Ward, told the Commons: 'As a result of the test firings which have taken place in the USA and in light of the progress made in the training programme we are now satisfied that Thor is able to take its place as part of the operational front line of the Royal Air Force.'[10]

A major problem was whether narrow, twisty East Anglia roads and lanes could accommodate 65ft-long missiles, on their transporter erector launcher (TEL) vehicles, being driven from the airhead to their launch bases. The manufacturers were asked to modify the transporters to incorporate steering on both rear wheels; this meant they required three drivers but were marginally more manoeuvrable. Tests were carried out on the taxiways at Lakenheath, which were laid out with oil drums to simulate the narrow roads and tight bends. In some cases, road signs had to be moved or taken down, vegetation cut back, even roads widened or strengthened to allow the massive convoys to safely negotiate access routes to the five regional bases.

When the East Anglian complex had been fully equipped, its missiles in place and warheads fitted, and its RAF crews had completed their training in the States, the first ever strategic missile squadrons in the free world were put on what was essentially a war footing – ready to launch at fifteen minutes' notice, twenty-four hours a day, 365 days a year. Initially, Bomber Command's policy was to have 60 per cent (or thirty-six) of the missiles available for firing at all times. This eventually increased to 75 per cent, but even at 60 per cent the strategic missiles deployed in the east of England accounted for a far more potent strike threat than the fourteen V-bombers which were always kept armed with nuclear bombs at an equivalent state of readiness on the RAF's operational V-bomber bases.

The Cuban Missile Crisis in October 1962 put the Thor missiles to their greatest test. Khrushchev, having seen the Americans station Thor intermediate range nuclear missiles in the UK, and Jupiter intermediate-missiles in Turkey and Italy, decided he would follow suit. He covertly deployed Russian intermediate- and medium-range missiles to Cuba, together with Cruise missiles and tactical nuclear weapons. In Cuba, the USSR had a platform from which it could threaten nuclear strikes on most American cities. Khrushchev's view was, why shouldn't the USSR turn the tables on America by adopting a similar policy of forward deployment?

When President Kennedy discovered what his adversary was doing, the two major powers of East and West squared up to each other, and the Cold War entered its most dangerous few days. The readiness of America's Strategic Air Command was raised twice, ultimately to 'Defence Condition Two', just one step below all-out war. On the critical weekend of 27–28 October, Bomber Command's V-Force and its Thor missiles were secretly placed on the UK's equivalent, 'Alert Three'. It meant that nuclear deterrent forces on both sides of the Atlantic were poised at their highest states of readiness in the whole of the Cold War years, and the world was closer than it had ever been to nuclear war.

RAF launch crews in East Anglia, and elsewhere down the east of England, brought fifty-nine of the sixty missiles to within fifteen minutes or less of the 'war/peace' keys being turned. When Kennedy and Khrushchev finally reached agreement, within hours of Kennedy launching a threatened invasion of Cuba, there was a secret understanding that America would withdraw its Jupiter missiles from Turkey.

Although, in the eyes of many in the RAF, the Cuban Missile Crisis had proved Thor's worth, the United States and British governments had already agreed to a gradual rundown of the Thor bases. The five East Anglian missile squadrons were disbanded in July 1963. As far as the Americans were concerned, their intercontinental missiles, Minuteman and Titan, had made Thor bases in the UK superfluous. Britain had hoped to replace Thor with its own nuclear missile, Blue Streak, but development of the weapon had been halted in 1960 because of technical difficulties and the spiralling cost.

So, the demise of Thor ended the RAF's brief missile era, and the strategic missile squadrons, nicknamed disparagingly 'Penguin Squadrons' by some in the service because they were 'all flap and no fly', were wound up.

That was not the view of Air Marshal Sir Kenneth Cross, commander-in-chief of Bomber Command, under whose command the Thor force operated. In an order of the day sent to all strategic missile squadrons, he wrote:

You in the Thor Force have maintained a constant vigil day and night for almost four years. You have maintained a higher state of readiness in peacetime than has ever been achieved before in the history of the armed forces of the Crown. I am well aware of the sacrifices, so willingly accepted, that this constant readiness has imposed on the officers and airmen of the Force. I am content that history will recognise your devoted service in the cause of peace. I know that I can rely on you for the same devotion during the rundown period as you have shown since the birth of the force in 1958.[11]

Meanwhile, Roland Hall had been seconded to the team designing the proposed underground silos for the ill-fated Blue Streak rocket – Britain's own nuclear missile that was to have succeeded Thor and provided the UK with its own entirely independent missile force. The expertise he had shown in preparing the drawings needed to get the Thor launch pads fast-tracked to an operational stage was devoted in 1959 to designing multi-floored underground silos that would have housed and protected Blue Streak and its launch crews.

Whereas Thor was vulnerable and could not be concealed or launched from below ground, Blue Streak, had it ever reached an operational stage, would have been fired direct from its concealed underground shelter. The silos had to overcome several problems. First, they had to withstand a 1-megaton explosion from an incoming Soviet missile strike within ½ mile, so the silo outer walls were designed to be built of 5ft thick reinforced concrete and encased in half an inch of mild steel. The electromagnetic effects of a nuclear explosion threatened to be as damaging to the missile's technology as the blast, so the top of the silo was to be sealed by a massive rail-mounted concrete lid weighing 400 tons. There also had to be a way of enabling the huge rush of hot gases to escape safely when the rocket was launched. This was achieved by allowing the gases to exit via a U-shaped shaft directed away from the rest of the silo. Finally, there had to be a means of combating the massive reverberation generated when the firing process took place. This was to be overcome by incorporating a special acoustic lining to the silo.

Had Blue Streak ever been fully developed, the building of silos would have represented a hugely expensive civil engineering project. It was assumed that, for the same fear of risk to the UK population that dictated that the Thor launch emplacements were built in East Anglia and down the east of England, the sixty Blue Streak silos would have followed a similar pattern of locations, with East Anglia again in the 'firing line'. Indeed, trial boreholes were drilled at Duxford in Cambridgeshire and other locations in the region to test the viability of locating silos in East Anglia.

The plan was to build the silos in groups of five or ten, associated with a technical and domestic complex spaced at sufficient intervals to ensure that only one silo in any group could be destroyed by a 20-megaton incoming warhead. The possibility of using some disused Rotor bunkers, like that at Bawburgh just outside Norwich, was contemplated.

The interior of the silos in Roland Hall's drawings showed seven floors underground. The fuel storage tanks would have been at the bottom; with plant rooms, storage areas, servicing bays, and launch crew and control rooms accommodated on the higher floors. The plans that were drawn up were as unique at the time as those for Thor had been. They showed how the first underground hot-launch missile facility could be effected, a plan adopted in America for its second generation of Titan intercontinental missiles. It is not surprising that, facing technical problems with its development and escalating costs, the British Government realised that Blue Streak was unaffordable. Each silo, and sixty of them were planned, was reckoned to cost nearly £500,000 to build at 1960 prices, and each missile with its warhead estimated at £3 million. Blue Streak was the missile Britain never built, and in June 1969, with the introduction of Polaris, responsibility for the UK's nuclear deterrent transferred from the RAF to the Royal Navy.

NOTES

1   Interview with Roland Hall, July 2009.
2   Deputy Chief of Air Staff's memo to ministers, January 1958; Humphrey Wynn, RAF Nuclear Deterrent Forces (London: HMSO, 1944) pp. 288–89.
3   East Anglian Daily Times, 'East Anglia is Sitting Target: Peer on extreme peril of Nuclear Attack', 12 February 1959.
4   White Paper, 21 February 1958.
5   PRO, AIR 20/10555. Letter from C-in-C Bomber Command to DCAS, 27 Feb 1958.
6   Chiefs of Staff meeting, 20 May 1957.
7   Portanova, Dr Peter L., and Dr L. Parker Temple, 'Project Emily and Thor IRBM in the United Kingdom 1955–1960', Air Power History, September 2009.
8   Ibid.
9   Commons Questions, 9 December 1959.
10 Boyes, John, Project Emily: Thor IRBM and the RAF (Stroud: Tempus, 2008), p. 93.
11 'Order of the Day' from C-in-C Bomber Command, Air Marshal Sir Kenneth Cross, 2 August 1962.

RAF Vulcans of the V-Force under guard and at readiness on an East Anglian operational airfield. (Author's collection)

Part of the declassified, but still heavily redacted, Murphy-Dean Agreement detailing the 'understandings' between US and UK governments for the use by the Americans of strategic bases on British sovereign territory. (US National Security Archives)

REPORT TO THE PRESIDENT AND THE PRIME MINISTER

Subject: Procedures for the Committing to the Attack of Nuclear Retaliatory Forces in the United Kingdom

1. Pursuant to the suggestion made by the Prime Minister to the President on April 24, 1958, representatives of the United States and United Kingdom Governments, led respectively by Mr. Robert Murphy and Sir Patrick Dean, have met in Washington. They studied how procedures of the two Governments might be concerted for reaching a decision to respond to a Soviet attack by committing nuclear retaliatory forces to the attack from the United Kingdom. The present report summarizes the results of these talks.

2. The basic understanding between the United Kingdom and United States Governments, regarding the use of bases in the United Kingdom by United States forces, provides that such use in an emergency shall be a matter for joint decision by the two Governments in the light of the circumstances at the time. A similar provision is incorporated in the Agreement of February 22, 1958, pursuant to which certain intermediate range ballistic missiles are to be provided to the United Kingdom Government by the United States Government. Decision by both parties would also be required in order to commit to the attack aircraft of the Royal Air Force Medium Bomber Force carrying nuclear weapons ████████.

3. If Western retaliation is to be successful, there must be mutually understood procedures for ordering the retaliatory forces referred to in paragraph 2 above into action with the minimum delay.

4. An outline of United Kingdom procedures is attached at Annex A, and an outline of United States procedures at Annex B. Representatives of the two Governments are satisfied that these procedures, which are designed to be put into effect with the minimum delay, are mutually understood and mutually consistent.

It will

THE DIVISION OF CLASSIFICATION, U.S. ENERGY RESEARCH AND DEVELOPMENT ADMINISTRATION, HAS DETERMINED THAT THIS DOCUMENT CONTAINS NO RESTRICTED DATA OR FORMERLY RESTRICTED DATA. ERDA HAS NO OBJECTION TO ITS DECLASSIFICATION.

SANITIZED COPY
SENSITIVE INFORMATION DELETED

PARTIALLY DECLASSIFIED
MR NLE 92-307 Doc 1
By ____

NARA Date 1/23/96

TOP SECRET

Left: Lt Col 'Hack' Mixson (left), the American co-ordinator of the highly secret reconnaissance flights flown over the Soviet Union from RAF Sculthorpe in the early 1950s, with Sqd Ldr John Crampton DFC, AFC, commander of the RAF's shadowy 'Special Duties Flight' and (right) Flt Lt Rex Sanders, his navigator. (US Air Force photo)

Below: American RB-45C aircraft, the planes that overflew the USSR, painted with RAF roundels, lined up at RAF Sculthorpe in Norfolk, at the time the USAF's largest airbase in Europe. (US Air Force photo)

One of the distinctive 'pagoda' buildings erected at the Atomic Weapons Research Establishment's offshoot at Orford Ness for the testing of the UK's first nuclear weapons. (Photograph courtesy of C.M. Glee)

Top left: 'Blue Danube', the UK's first nuclear weapon. Measuring 24ft in length and 5ft in diameter, it weighed 10,000lbs and had a nominal yield of between 10 and 12 kilotons. (Courtesy of Keith Eldred)

Top right: The Barnham nuclear bomb store as it looked from the air in the late 1950s. The three main bomb storage units and the four 'sprigs' of nuclear core storage 'huts' can be clearly seen, together with the sterile security surrounding the pentagon's five sides. (Author's collection)

One of the fifty-seven nuclear core storage sheds at the Barnham bomb store, showing the high level of security for the first generation of the UK's nuclear weapons. In the background is part of the concrete security wall and beyond one of the five watchtowers which guard the site. (Photograph courtesy of Sam Tolley)

One of three bomb storage units built at Barnham for the UK's first independent nuclear weapons. They are protected by solid blast mounds and have a gantry at the entrance to lift bombs and bomb components into the storage area. (Photograph courtesy of Sam Tolley)

Checking the flow of liquid oxygen into the missile on an RAF Thor launch pad in East Anglia. The super-cooled LOX can be seen 'boiling off' as a vapour cloud. (Photograph courtesy of Sqd Ldr Frank Leatherdale)

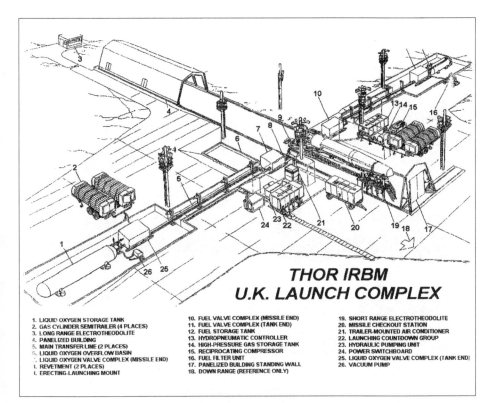

THOR IRBM
U.K. LAUNCH COMPLEX

1. LIQUID OXYGEN STORAGE TANK
2. GAS CYLINDER SEMITRAILER (4 PLACES)
3. LONG RANGE ELECTROTHEODOLITE
4. PANELIZED BUILDING
5. MAIN TRANSFER LINE (2 PLACES)
6. LIQUID OXYGEN OVERFLOW BASIN
7. LIQUID OXYGEN VALVE COMPLEX (MISSILE END)
8. REVETMENT (2 PLACES)
9. ERECTING-LAUNCHING MOUNT

10. FUEL VALVE COMPLEX (MISSILE END)
11. FUEL VALVE COMPLEX (TANK END)
12. FUEL STORAGE TANK
13. HYDROPNEUMATIC CONTROLLER
14. HIGH-PRESSURE GAS STORAGE TANK
15. RECIPROCATING COMPRESSOR
16. FUEL FILTER UNIT
17. PANELIZED BUILDING STANDING WALL
18. DOWN RANGE (REFERENCE ONLY)

19. SHORT RANGE ELECTROTHEODOLITE
20. MISSILE CHECKOUT STATION
21. TRAILER-MOUNTED AIR CONDITIONER
22. LAUNCHING COUNTDOWN GROUP
23. HYDRAULIC PUMPING UNIT
24. POWER SWITCHBOARD
25. LIQUID OXYGEN VALVE COMPLEX (TANK END)
26. VACUUM PUMP

The layout of one of East Anglia's fifteen nuclear missile launch pads as built to the detailed technical drawings produced by Roland Hall for Project Emily. (Author's collection)

Thor rockets were not built to negotiate narrow rural roads in East Anglia. The transporter/erector vehicles had to be modified with rear-wheel steering to enable them to reach launch sites in the East Anglian countryside. (Author's collection)

The Cambridge War Room from which, had nuclear conflict broken out, East Anglia would have been governed by a Commissioner of Cabinet rank, exercising a draconian form of regional rule. (Photograph courtesy of Nick Catford)

An inoffensive-looking bungalow sits on top of the bunker at Bawburgh on the outskirts of Norwich. It was originally built as the headquarters for the air defence of the Eastern Region as part of the Rotor system. Later the bunker was adapted as regional government headquarters for East Anglia. (Photograph courtesy of Nick Catford)

The Norwich headquarters of No. 6 Group ROC to which the UK Warning and Motoring Organisation in bunkers across East Anglia would have reported in time of nuclear war. (Photograph courtesy of Nick Catford)

One of more than 100 small subterranean bunkers built across East Anglia from which nuclear bursts and fallout would have been monitored by volunteer ROC members had the Cold War led to Armageddon. (Author's collection)

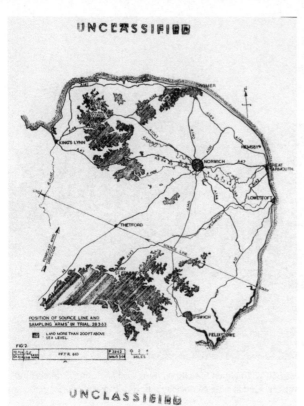

A declassified map showing the flight line across Suffolk and Norfolk from where simulated germ-war agents were released to drift in the wind across Norwich during secret experiments undertaken by scientists from the Chemical Defence Establishment at Porton Down in 1964. (Porton Field Trial Report No. 610)

A declassified map showing the sampling positions in and around Norwich where levels of zinc cadmium sulphide, sprayed from an aircraft, were monitored in germ warfare tests carried out on unsuspecting Norwich residents. (Porton Field Trial Report No. 610)

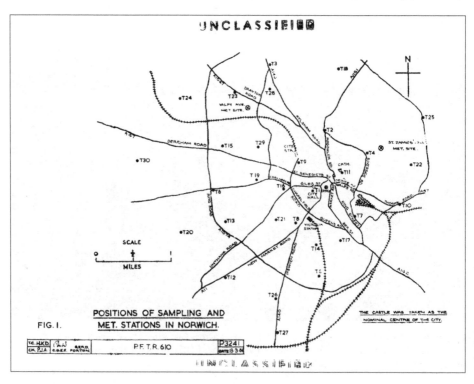

The vast aerial array for 'Cobra Mist' built at Orford Ness on the Suffolk coast in the early 1970s to peer into Soviet airspace. The huge fan-shaped antenna covered 135 acres. (US National Security Archives)

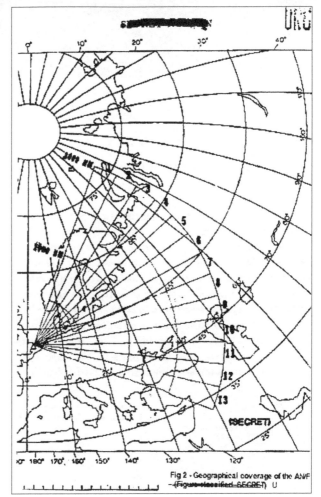

A declassified map showing the prospective reach of 'Cobra Mist' – well behind the Iron Curtain. (US National Security Archives)

Fig 2 - Geographical coverage of the ANF - (Figure classified SECRET) U

US Mark 6 fission bomb. Three of these weapons, each with a yield ten times the bomb dropped on Hiroshima, were in the igloo torn apart at RAF Lakenheath when a B-47 ploughed into it in July 1956. (US Air Force photo)

LGA185 CBA9 95

OO RJEDMH

DE RJDLGB 97

O 272114Z ZFF1

TOP SECRET

OPERATIONAL IMMEDIATE

ACTION

INFO

FM COMAIRDIV 7 USAB SOUTH RUISLIP ENGLAND

TO CINCSAC OFFUTT AFB NEBR

T O P S E C R E T /COMDR T-5262. PERSONAL FOR CINC LEMAY FROM VALSH. MORE TO MY PHONE CALL. HAVE JUST COME FROM THE VRECKAGE OF B-47 WHICH PLOUGHED INTO AN IGLOO IN LAKENHEATH ADS. THE B-47 TORE APART THE IGLOO AND KNOCKED ABOUT 3 MARK SIXES. A/C THEN EXPLODED SHOWERING BURNING FUEL OVERALL. CREW PERISHED. MOST OF A/C VRECKAGE PIVOTED ON IGLOO AND CAME TO REST WITH A/C NOSE JUST BEYOND IGLOO BANK VHICH KEPT MAIN FUEL FIRE OUTSIDE SMASHED IGLOO. PRELIMINARY EXAM BY BOMB DISPOSAL OFFICER SAYS A MIRACLE THAT ONE MARK SIX WITH EXPOSED DETONATORS SHEARED DIDN'T GO. FIRE FIGHTERS EXTINGUISHED FIRE AROUND MARK SIXES FAST. PLAN INVESTIGATION TO VARRANT DECORATING FIREMEN.

B T

27/2138Z JUL RJDLGB

This document consists of......

Copy No......... of ....

reproduction of this message in hole or in part is prohibited ... roval of ADJUTANT.

The telegram sent from the US Air Force Commander in the UK to General Curtis LeMay reporting on the crash in July 1956 in which a B-47 ploughed into a nuclear bomb store. He comments that it was 'a miracle one Mark Six with exposed detonators didn't go'. (Declassified from LeMay papers, US Library of Congress)

A Thor missile launch crew line up in front of their rocket on an East Anglian launch pad. Note at front left the American Authentication Officer, who held the key to arm the nuclear warhead, and his RAF colleague to the right, who held the key to initiate the launch process. (Author's collection)

From its launch pads in East Anglia, a Thor missile could carry a 1.45-megaton warhead to Moscow in eighteen minutes. The UK Government knew that as a result of locating rocket bases in East Anglia it made the region a prime target for the Soviet Union. (Photograph courtesy of Ian Killick)

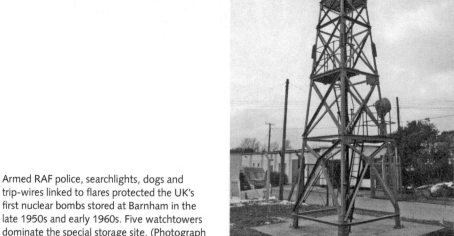

Armed RAF police, searchlights, dogs and trip-wires linked to flares protected the UK's first nuclear bombs stored at Barnham in the late 1950s and early 1960s. Five watchtowers dominate the special storage site. (Photograph courtesy of Sam Tolley)

5

LIFE BEYOND THE BOMB

IF THE TEMPERATURE of the Cold War had risen and nuclear attack had become a reality, East Anglia, like the rest of the country, would have been placed under a draconian form of government – regional rule by a government minister, of Cabinet rank, in sole charge of his personal fiefdom, safe in a supposedly secure bunker. The unimaginable horror of life beyond the bomb comes across in grim studies carried out in the secrecy of Whitehall – documents that were not made public until more than a decade after the end of the Cold War.

In the early 1950s, work began on building these regional headquarters. East Anglia's was located at Cambridge, and construction was virtually completed by 1953. The new buildings cost close to £1 million each, plus another £700,000 for the complex plant with which they were fitted to allow a large number of people to live and work there for a number of weeks, supplied with their own power, water supplies and communications.

The Cambridge 'bunker' was conveniently sited at Brooklands Avenue. Like many others around the UK, it was part of the government estate where regional offices of various ministries were based. The logic was that each department of government would provide officials to staff the wartime centre and support the Regional Commissioner in his task of maintaining some kind of order out of the chaos and misery of nuclear conflict. The downside of placing it among other government buildings was that the location was obvious to anyone familiar with the pattern of devolved central government.

Protection against nuclear attack was poor. The building was 'semi-sunken' and therefore offered puny shelter against the blast and heat of thermo-nuclear weapons, even though its walls were constructed of reinforced concrete almost 5ft thick and it was topped with a roof of similar strength. It was surrounded by a 10ft security fence capped with barbed wire. A filtra-tion system offered some protection against nuclear fallout and chemical or biological attack, but the building itself would never have withstood the dev-astating effects of a nuclear bomb dropped on or over the city of Cambridge. And, with several prime military targets relatively close by, it was inevitable that the Soviets would aim to hit East Anglia hard – probably harder than any other part of the UK other than London.

In August 1953 the Soviet Union detonated its first H-bomb, and planners within Whitehall, whose task was to work out how to ensure the survival of the nation in a war that would bring death and destruction on an unimagina-ble scale, needed to reappraise their plans. It was recognised that, if nuclear conflict became a reality, the wholesale devastation that would follow would mean the recovery period – if indeed recovery was ever possible – would extend for much longer than was previously envisaged. Regions would have to govern themselves autonomously for weeks, perhaps even months. The fear expressed by civil servants and scientists, but kept from the public so as not to undermine morale, was of a society collapsing in on itself and the total shattering of the rule of law. Civil defence, as it had been understood in the Second World War, was useless, unaffordable and probably unworkable in the scenario of total nuclear war. The government's key issues were a belief that nuclear deterrence was the best defence against attack, and the con-viction that maintaining the machinery of government, even if devolved to regions, would enable some semblance of organised society to emerge from the wreckage of a nuclear winter.

In 1955, Churchill asked Sir William Strath, a civil servant in the Central War Plans Secretariat, to lead a top secret study into the effects of a thermonuclear attack on the UK. The findings were so apocalyptic that Churchill ordered the report must be suppressed. It was not declassified until April 2002. Strath concluded, from the latest intelligence available, that a Soviet assault would have three main objectives: first, to destroy those air-fields in East Anglia hosting US or British bombers; second, to destroy the British Government; and third, to render the UK useless as a base for any form of military operations.

In 1955, Strath's conclusions would have made grim reading for anyone living in East Anglia. He stated that in a built-up area like Cambridge or

Norwich the heat flash from a hydrogen bomb would cause up to 100,000 fires in a circumference of around 60–100 miles. He calculated that just ten hydrogen bombs could blanket most of the UK with radioactive fall-out. Almost one third of the British population would be killed or injured immediately, and most of the nation's farmland would be rendered unusable for many months – some of the most productive land could be lost for generations – and supplies of drinking water would be contaminated beyond use.

In a section of his findings entitled 'Machinery of Control', Strath warned that society would collapse in much of the UK. Civil order would have to be restored through 'rough and ready methods'. The surviving population would face an appalling struggle 'against disease, starvation, and unimaginable psychological effects of nuclear bombardment'.

Churchill ordered the BBC not to broadcast news about the hydrogen bomb that might discourage the public. Telling the truth about nuclear weapons, the British Government feared, would weaken public support for a defence policy that required the UK to have them in its arsenal.[1]

It was in a direct response to the Strath Report that the government built a massive bunker in the Wiltshire countryside, to act as an alternative seat of central government should a nuclear world war occur. Hidden inside a limestone quarry, it was large enough to provide more than 1 million ft^2 of accommodation and cater for several thousand people. During the height of the Cold War it was known by various code names: Subterfuge, Burlington, Turnstile, Chanticleer, Eyeglass and Peripheral among them.

The locations of most of the early regional war rooms were reorganised when the potential horrors of the Soviet Union using H-bombs were better understood. In most cases, the more vulnerable war rooms were replaced with hardened deep bunkers. But, despite the vulnerability of East Anglia, the East Midlands and Lincolnshire because of their proximity to multiple targets, the war rooms at Cambridge and Nottingham remained in their existing, far from adequate, semi-sunken buildings. Maybe it indicated an acceptance by central government that the list of prime Soviet targets in the east of England was so great that obliteration of swathes of these regions was inevitable – so realistic protection for regional government in England's eastern counties was undeliverable. In any case, by the middle of 1963 the Soviets would have been well aware where the regional centres of government were located. 'Spies for Peace', part of the CND movement, had distributed a detailed list during the protest march to the Atomic Weapons Research Establishment at Aldermaston that year.

In the early 1960s, the Cambridge regional centre of government was extended to accommodate around 400 people with the addition of a large two-storey surface bunker,[2] but the extra space was constructed with even less robust walls than the original structure, so there was little possibility of its survival had the Soviets attacked targets in the Cambridge area. The dormitories and dining facilities were in the most vulnerable part of the building, where even protection against radiation was uncertain.

The government was painfully aware of the danger to public morale if nuclear conflict become a reality, and the most important figures in the region were provided with shelter while the rest of the population was left to face the prospect in rudimentary shelters, which much derided government information leaflets suggested could be hastily cobbled together using household doors and materials found in the home. Central government had ruled out the provision of nuclear shelters for the public as totally unaffordable. To build shelters just for the 11 million key workers who would be required to keep the country running would have cost £32 million, more than the entire NHS budget.[3]

In a nuclear conflict, people had to understand that they would be left to their own devices. A 1963 statement in the House of Commons acknowledged that eleven Regional Seats of Government (RSGs) had been built, but insisted that their purpose was 'not of protecting the occupants, but enabling succour and relief to be brought to the public after an attack to be carried out to the best advantage and to marshal services and supplies essential for survival'.[4]

Door signs which survive in the Cambridge bunker indicate that the staff, who would have been required to leave their families and take their chances in spartan accommodation, would have been split into distinct units: those responsible for public information, including the BBC, which had a small studio from which survivors in the region would receive instructions, providing they had access to a battery-powered radio; police and emergency service controllers; and a communications section. There was also accommodation for military liaison officers, and for senior officials overseeing utility services, in particular the distribution of medical supplies, water and food.

Central to the bunker was a two-storey operations room, dominated by a large map of the region on which the scale of the nuclear strike would have been plotted. Facing the operations room were glass-fronted offices from which the Regional Commissioner and his senior officers would be expected to manage the mayhem around them. In the words of the Hall Report in 1953, the Regional Commissioner would inevitably be needed 'to take over the reins of government from the shattered central administration'.[5]

Two years later, the Strath Report had looked in detail at the consequences of thermonuclear, as opposed to atomic, warfare and assessed in the grimmest of terms the UK's ability to survive a nuclear attack. It stated bluntly that ideas of civil defence would be largely irrelevant, and all resources would now have to be directed to the struggle for survival directed by the Regional Commissioners, possibly with some direction from the 'embunkered nucleus of central government' hidden in 'The Quarry' at Corsham. The whereabouts of the vast network of bunkers and tunnels for the prime minister and his senior advisers was one of the Cold War's most highly protected secrets.

The grim facts of thermonuclear war were spelt out in a secret memorandum to the minister of defence, Harold Macmillan, dated December 1954. 'In a war the United Kingdom – the nerve centre of European resistance – would be extremely vulnerable to attack. There is not in sight any air defence system which could protect us effectively. In short, possession by the West of the nuclear weapon is at present a real deterrent. Overwhelming and immediate retaliation with it is our only reliable defence.'[6]

The memo went on to highlight the grave effects of radioactive contamination that thermonuclear war posed for a country the size of the UK, and the immense problems it posed for the medical services and, a major concern for East Anglia, for agriculture.

A year later, the Joint Intelligence Committee (JIC) came up with a chilling report on the H-bomb threat, highlighting the particular vulnerability of East Anglia and the eastern region.[7] It listed Soviet objectives in a nuclear conflict as:

a)   To knock out as quickly as possible those airfields from which nuclear attacks could be launched on the Soviet Union.

b)   To destroy the organisation of government and control.

c)   To render the UK useless as a base for any form of military operations.

The JIC report ended with an alarming addendum, which contained a particularly grim message for East Anglia, where both British and US nuclear deterrent units were largely located: 'We believe the Russians will regard the UK as such a threat that they will aim to render it unusable for a long period, and will not hesitate to destroy great parts of the UK to achieve this aim.'

The Cabinet Office committee tasked to wrestle with the appalling vision of a war in which the country was attacked by multiple hydrogen bombs was the Central War Plans Secretariat. The group's report made sober reading:

A successful night attack on the main centres of population in this country with ten hydrogen bombs would, we estimate, kill about 12 million people and seriously injure or disable 4 million others. Casualties on such a scale would be intolerable; they would mean the loss of nearly one third of the population; they would moreover include a disproportionate share of the skilled manpower on which our future would depend.[8]

The grim statistics suggested that, as well as those killed, around 13–27 million would die slowly and painfully from radiation sickness, with virtually no chance of medical relief. It is no wonder that the stark facts in the Strath Report were concealed from the British people until 2002.

A government assessment of probable nuclear targets in the UK, drawn up in the 1960s, pulled no punches as to the vulnerability of East Anglia. It listed some sixteen strategic targets in the region that were almost certainly on the USSR's prime targets list.[9] It recognised that strikes would include the regional seat of government at Cambridge; V-bomber bases at Wittering (Cambridgeshire), Wyton (Huntingdonshire), Honington (Suffolk) and Marham (Norfolk); American bases at Lakenheath, Bentwaters and Woodbridge (Suffolk), and Alconbury (Cambridgeshire); and fighter bases at Coltishall (Norfolk) and Wattisham (Suffolk). It also anticipated nuclear attacks on West Raynham (Norfolk) to eliminate the surface to air missiles based there, and radar sites at Neatishead and Feltwell (Norfolk), together with Bawdsey and Orford Ness (Suffolk). Had the Soviet Union carried out such a comprehensive attack on this number of targets, there is little doubt that East Anglia would have been reduced to a wasteland from which it is impossible to imagine any kind of recovery.

Who, then, would have had the unenviable task of becoming East Anglia's Regional Commissioner faced with the prospect of his region's almost total destruction? No comprehensive list exists, probably because ministers would not have been told their fate until 'transition to war' had been officially accepted by the Cabinet. But some names have been revealed in declassified official papers. In 1961, a year before the Cuban Missile Crisis came close to making all this a terrible reality, the minister scheduled to take control of the eastern region was the minister of labour, John Hare, the MP for Sudbury and Woodbridge.[10] By the summer of 1966, when the Wilson government had taken over from Harold Macmillan's Conservative administration, the former trade union leader Frank Cousins, by then in the Cabinet as minister of technology, was nominated for the Cambridge 'hot' seat.[11] Had the Cambridge bunker been manned, the prime minister and his most senior colleagues would have retreated to the British Government's final central redoubt, deep below Box Hill at Corsham in Wiltshire, known in Whitehall as 'the Quarry'.

The Regional Commissioner overseeing East Anglia would have exercised massive powers. A government report, dated 1955, stated: 'To maintain control under nuclear attack would require the use of drastic emergency powers … rough and ready methods would be needed to cover the period when the nation would be struggling to survive.' After the Cuban Missile Crisis scare in October 1962, when Harold Macmillan's government found itself unexpectedly facing the very real possibility of nuclear conflict and Britain's deterrent forces were placed on their highest alert in the whole of the Cold War, an Emergency Powers (Defence) Bill was drafted which would have granted Regional Commissioners draconian rights.

The draft bill was held in reserve, ready to be rushed through both Houses of Parliament in the final days of peace.[12] It gave Regional Commissioners, like the minister put in charge of East Anglia, extensive powers over life, property, the distribution of food and finance. So all-embracing were the powers envisaged, that the bill would have passed rights to the Regional Commissioners which would have amounted 'to a voluntary abdication by Parliament of the whole of its functions for the period of the emergency'. It is difficult to contemplate what other powers over life, liberty and property the Regional Commissioners might have been invested with, so all-embracing were those it was planned to grant them. A 'special circumstances' sub-section of the bill can be interpreted to mean anything the Regional Commissioner wanted it to mean once the bill had gained the force of law. Indeed, the ferocity of the draft measures was so great it was thought prudent to keep it firmly under wraps during peacetime. Granting such sweeping legislative powers over life and death to a single politician could only have been palatable under the threat of nuclear war. No one outside the secret state of Whitehall had sight of these drastic proposals, until the draft bill was declassified and the file containing its details released to the Public Record Office in the late 1990s.

The ministers, like John Hare, who became Viscount Blakenham, taking his title from the name of a Suffolk village, would have been appointed to their Regional Commissioner roles by Royal Warrant. Ready-printed warrants were prepared, duly signed by the Queen, so that the necessary constitutional process could be adhered to as the shadow of a nuclear world war approached. The grand legal language in these documents chimes oddly with the grim circumstances for which they were prepared:[13]

> Elizabeth the Second, by the Grace of God of the United Kingdom of Great
> Britain and Northern Ireland and Our other Realms and Territories, Queen,
> Head of the Commonwealth, Defender of the Faith to our [Minister's name]
> Greeting! In pursuance of Regulation 4 (2) of the Defence (Machinery
> of Government) Regulations we hereby appoint you, the said [Minister's
> name] to be Regional Commissioner for the purposes of those Regulations.
> Granted at Our Court of St James's ? day of 19?? In the ? year of our Reign.
> By Her Majesty's Command.

So, even with the UK perhaps facing a nuclear winter from which it may
never have recovered, the formalities of constitutional monarchy were preserved. The newly sworn-in Regional Commissioner for East Anglia would
have been handed a sealed envelope and told to head for his bunker at
Cambridge, leaving his wife and family to their own fate. One very senior
police officer, who knew that if the worst happened he was among those
destined to take a place in the region's bunker, told me that when the chips
were down he doubted he could have deserted his wife and family. One
wonders how many, in those horrifying circumstances, would have had similar thoughts.

The envelope from the Cabinet Office, handed to the Regional Commissioner
for East Anglia, would have given detailed guidance for his role:[14]

> You should be ready to take up your appointment at short notice (if you
> have not already been notified by telephone of your appointment and
> asked to proceed to your emergency station before these notes reach you).
> When a Proclamation is made under the Defence Act, or the attack takes
> place, extensive powers will devolve on you in your own right as Regional
> Commissioner. You will then exercise all the existing powers and emergency
> powers of government within your region, except those reserved to the
> Central government but including control of the Armed Forces and you
> may, if the situation requires it, make new laws by Ordinance.

The guidance went on to explain that the Regional Commissioner would
be handed a copy of the *Government War Book* which would set out the
control systems at regional and sub-regional level, and provide details of
emergency powers, broadcasting and monitoring arrangements, communications, the administration of justice and even the distribution of money to
survivors, in the aftermath of a nuclear attack in order to stimulate the revival
of some kind of economic activity. The gravest concerns of the Regional

Commissioner, given ultimate power over his East Anglian fiefdom, would have been the total collapse of public morale that the Whitehall planners, trying to envisage how the nation could survive nuclear war, most feared. The Joint Inter-Services Group for the Study of All-Out War (JIGSAW) called this scenario, which they admitted was an all-too-possible outcome of an intensive Soviet attack, 'breakdown'. They defined 'breakdown' as occurring:

> When the government of a country is no longer able to ensure that its orders are carried out. This state of affairs could come about through breakdown of the machinery of control … or through the mass of people becoming preoccupied with their own survival rather than the country's war effort and prepared to run the risk of being shot rather than to obey orders which would seem to them to involve unreasonable personal risk, in a word, through the breakdown of morale.[15]

What an awful scenario for the Regional Commissioner to contemplate – exercising the power of life and death in an effort to sustain control and maintain order, in a situation where those who survived might truly envy the dead. An attack with thermonuclear bombs in the numbers the government's experts feared would almost certainly have caused more casualties than both world wars combined, and leave up to 21 million Britons dead, according to recently released archives.[16] Those who recall the government leaflets that were periodically distributed to households during those Cold War years, and the unrealistic advice they gave, were not wrong in suspecting that the civil defence structure that existed was little more than a smokescreen to bluff the public into passively accepting the nuclear arms race. Successive governments saw it, not so much as a practical attempt to ensure survival, as a political necessity to prevent the public from thinking atomic war equalled certain death. This was the dilemma at the heart of all Cold War civil defence planning. In terms of overall defence policy, civil defence was a necessary façade, and ministers knew it.

Nevertheless, the plans to try to ensure survival in East Anglia and the rest of the UK were in place. Just how realistic they were, and to what extent they could have been implemented, even given the draconian powers devolved to the Regional Commissioner should he and his staff survive it, is impossible to know.

As the Cold War dragged on, the government reviewed the structure of the regional seats of government and decided to divide the eastern region into two sub-areas. The war room for East Anglia was moved from the vulnerable semi-sunken building in Cambridge to the outskirts of Norwich, where the largest and strongest bunker in the region, indeed one of the largest in the country, built in the early 1950s as headquarters for air defence of the eastern sector, had become vacant.

What was originally RAF Bawburgh, a deep three-storey bunker located between what is now the city's woodland burial ground and the southern bypass, was converted in the late 1970s and early 1980s, and given an additional fourth floor to provide accommodation for the minister deputed to take command and control of East Anglia. A new sub-regional headquarters was built beneath a government office block in Hertford to serve the southern part of 'Region Four'. Together, the two sub-regional HQs constituted the wartime government centres for the administration of the whole of the eastern region. The old Cambridge war room was closed. Given the prominence of prime targets in East Anglia, Bawburgh offered much greater protection for the Regional Commissioner and his staff, although parts of the extension were only partially below ground level and therefore not fully blast-protected.

Hidden amongst trees, the only giveaway sign that the Bawburgh bunker exists at all are its communications mast and what appeared to be a conventional bungalow with an attractive veranda. Below the bungalow is the bunker, 65ft deep, with a veritable rabbit warren of offices on the floors surrounding, and looking down on the main operations room in the bunker's basement. Built in the early 1950s at considerable cost, Bawburgh was part of what was then termed the 'Rotor' air defence system.

In the 1950s the UK was divided into six separate sectors for defence against nuclear attack. The two sectors that covered the eastern and southern coasts of the UK were regarded as the most vulnerable. These were the sectors provided with the best protected underground headquarters.

The 1949 Cherry Report, compiled as the international climate worsened after the end of the Second World War and Communism under Stalin expanded into Eastern Europe, reviewed Britain's exposure to Soviet attack at a time when it was clear Russia was becoming a nuclear power.

The radar system that had helped Britain win the Battle of Britain was not well equipped to detect and track modern aircraft. The report recommended a substantial rationalisation of the network of 170 radar sites surviving from the Second World War, many of them located down England's east coast. It proposed a wholesale modernisation under the code name 'Rotor'. This rationalised the old wartime system, and concentrated Britain's radar defence on sixty-six sites. However, 'Rotor' maintained many of the main elements of command and control that had been used in the 1940s. The project was massive, and because one of the main threats was seen to be to the east coast, the Sector Headquarters at Bawburgh was provided with one of the strongest bunkers at the apex of the 'Rotor' hierarchy.

The harmless-looking bungalow sitting on top of the bunker served as access and guard room. It provided good security, since the only access to the bunker, apart from an escape hatch approached by a steel staircase and capped by a heavy steel door, was through the innocent-looking building. From the air it looked no more significant than a domestic dwelling. Underneath, approached via a long sloping tunnel, leading to massive steel blast doors, and culminating in a staircase serving the various floors, was the underground operations centre. Bawburgh's official description, when it was first built, was an 'R4 bunker'. Those in that category were among the most impressive underground structures built during the early part of the Cold War. It was designed to be safe against a direct hit by a 2,000lb armour piercing bomb, dropped from a height of 26,000ft, or a near miss from a 20-kiloton nuclear weapon. To protect against the effects of ground shock the bunker was cast as a monolithic ferroconcrete structure reinforced at 6in intervals with steel rods. The outer walls and roof were 10ft thick and an additional 14–15ft of earth was mounded on top. It had its own borehole for water supplies, its own generators and filtered air conditioning.

The Rotor project was one of the most comprehensive of all the defence building programmes during the Cold War. Across the country the construction of one-, two- and three-storey bunkers involved 350,000 tons of concrete, 20,000 tons of steel, and thousands of miles of telephone and telex connections. The Rotor infrastructure was estimated to have cost the country £24 million, at 1950s prices. Its associated radar and communications networks were estimated at a further £28 million. All this was achieved at a time when the country was struggling financially to overcome the economic aftermath of the Second World War.

Included in the Rotor programme for East Anglia was a two-storey (R3) underground operations centre at Neatishead. Its role was to provide the 'eyes and the ears' to prevent Soviet bombers intruding into UK airspace. During the Cold War, Neatishead was tracking Russian aircraft approaching or entering British airspace as frequently as three times a week – more, when the UK was involved in NATO exercises. Neatishead's task was to vector RAF fighter aircraft to intercept them.

As a young RAF national serviceman I was posted to work in the Bawburgh bunker in 1954, shortly after it had opened. The concept of air defence had not progressed far beyond the system of plotting Luftwaffe raids during the Blitz. The technology had improved, but the fundamentals of the process were similar. Aircraft were tracked by radar, and their course, height and numbers were communicated to the operations centre at Bawburgh, where their positions were displayed on a huge table-top map located at the base of the bunker. Plotters wielding magnetic poles used metal arrows to show the track of aircraft approaching the east coast, or moving across the region. A complete picture was actively built up as the data was communicated in real time from the radar stations to the earphones of the plotters. In the early 1950s jet fighters were commonplace on RAF fighter squadrons, replacing the piston-engined Spitfires and Hurricanes of the 1940s – otherwise, the whole operation was closely reminiscent of the days of the Battle of Britain.

Surrounding the plotting floor were tiers of glass-fronted offices from which senior RAF controllers deployed fighter aircraft and co-ordinated any response to potential incursions into UK airspace. It added up to a spectacular 'theatre of war' – RAF controllers in direct contact with their fighter squadrons, artillery officers controlling anti-aircraft batteries, and what was termed the 'tote wall' displaying the availability of squadrons on standby on airfields across the region.

Within a few years of the Rotor system and RAF Bawburgh becoming operational, two developments hit the project like a bombshell. First was the arrival of Type 80 Centrimetric Early Warning Radar, codenamed, in the rather eccentric lexicon of the Ministry of Defence, 'Green Garlic'. This changed the whole concept of fighter control. The new radar proved that it was far more efficient to control intercept fighters direct from the radar site. It cut out the inevitable delay caused by communicating data to Sector HQ before a response was launched. Speed was becoming the essence of air defence, and would become even more crucial when missiles replaced bombers and the totemic four-minute warning became the bogey of the Cold War. The first operational 'Green Garlic' radar went on line at RAF Trimingham in North Norfolk in 1955.

The next body blow to the Rotor system was the Soviet acquisition of the H-bomb, in November 1955, linked to the advent of high-flying supersonic bombers. Every second saved in identification and interception was vital. The Rotor system had been designed to deter a 400mph piston-engined bomber carrying an atomic bomb, but the new threat required a faster, slicker response. Much of the infrastructure of Rotor became redundant overnight.

Bawburgh was earmarked as the master control centre for the oversight of all military and civil aviation in the UK, under a new scheme entitled 'Linesman/Mediator'. The Bawburgh site was assessed and surveyed to accommodate a second three-storey bunker, alongside the existing one, with an entrance half way along the access tunnel to the first bunker. Government approval was given, and, had it been built, it would have made Bawburgh the most extensive and unique bunker in the UK. But, due to serious computer problems encountered on the 'Linesman' project, and Treasury objections to the cost (some £100 million), the plan was abandoned. In any case, when the Soviet Union began developing its missile arsenal, the concept of Bawburgh being the sole headquarters from which the UK air defence against Soviet nuclear bombers would be directed had itself become obsolete.

The Bawburgh bunker remained on a care-and-maintenance basis until, following the Cuban Missile Crisis of October 1962, the rethink on how to ensure national survival should nuclear war become a reality resulted in its selection as East Anglia's regional centre of government.

In 1966, the bunker at Neatishead was largely destroyed in a tragic fire in which three Norfolk civilian firemen lost their lives. The blaze was started deliberately, deep underground in a technical store, by a disaffected airman who set fire to piled-up papers. He was subsequently tried, convicted and sentenced to seven years' imprisonment.

Initially the RAF station's own fire service attempted to tackle the blaze. Fortunately all the personnel on duty were safely evacuated from the bunker. When the Norfolk Fire Service arrived, the bunker was almost impenetrably smoke logged. Faced with an extremely dangerous situation, Divisional Officer R. Dix entered the underground building with two of his colleagues, each of them wearing breathing apparatus. After thirty minutes, when the three had overstayed their allocated time, a rescue team went in search of them. They were able to locate two of the missing men, but not Dix. A second rescue team entered the bunker, and they too failed to find the Divisional Officer. A third search team found Dix and the other lost men, but on arrival at hospital Dix was pronounced dead. During these extremely brave rescue attempts it was discovered that two further firemen were missing. Final desperate attempts to find them and bring them out were defeated by heat and dense smoke. After the fire had been burning for some hours, and with all hope of a successful rescue gone, it was decided to flood the bunker as the only way of dousing the flames. The bodies of Leading Fireman H.J. Durrant and Fireman J.S. Holman were found after the bunker had been pumped out.

Tributes were paid to the three heroic Norfolk firemen in the House of Commons by the Secretary of State for Defence, Bruce Millan, when he announced a Royal Air Force Board of Inquiry into the disaster.[17] The MP for

North Norfolk, Mr Bert Hazell, challenged the minister about lack of breathing apparatus for the civilian firemen, asking if it was true that the first crew on the scene were not equipped with breathing apparatus and sets had to be obtained from the Norwich City Brigade, with a consequent delay.

Six months later, following the Air Force Board inquiry, a further statement in the Commons disclosed that as a result of the Neatishead fire all RAF bunkers were being examined with the aim of reducing fire risks, and liaison between the RAF and local fire authorities was being strengthened, and would include frequent familiarisation visits and on-site exercises.[18] A small committee under the chairmanship of the Chief Inspector of Fire Services was convened to review firefighting operations in underground premises.

Meanwhile, the radars installed at Neatishead remained in use, the data they collected being relayed to other command and control sites. Fortunately, when the fire occurred Neatishead was undergoing a periodic maintenance, so the UK's air defences were not affected by closure of the bunker. The station did not regain its operational role until 1973, when a new radar control centre was opened in a building originally used in the Second World War. This centre remained in use, with frequent upgrades to install more sophisticated electronics, until 1993. It now forms the centrepiece of the Royal Air Force Air Defence Museum, which tells the story of radar and its importance in both the Second World War and the Cold War. The Bawburgh site is now in private hands, owned by a communications company.

NOTES

1   TNA, PRO, CAB 134/940. Strath Report, March 1955.
2   Cocroft, Wayne D. & Roger J.C. Thomas, *Cold War: Building for Nuclear Confrontation 1946–1989* (London: English Heritage, 2003).
3   Grant, Matthew, *After the Bomb: Civil Defence and Nuclear War in Britain* (Basingstoke: Palgrave Macmillan, 2010).
4   Parliamentary statement, 27 June 1963, Hansard, Vol. 679 Col. 1842.
5   Hall Report 1953: 'Strengthening the Machinery of Government in a Nuclear War', quoted in Grant, *After the Bomb*.
6   TNA, PRO, DEFE 13/45. Macmillan to Churchill, 13 December 1954.
7   TNA, PRO, CAB 158/20 JIC (55), 12, 13 January 1955.
8   TNA, PRO, CAB 134/940HDC (55) 3.
9   Annexe A to COS 1929/2/11/67: 'Probable Targets in the United Kingdom, Assumptions for Planning'.
10 TNA, PRO, CAB 21/6081. Appendix to Cabinet Secretary's memo to Macmillan, 13 September 1961.

11 TNA, PRO, PREM13/3565. 'Defence. Machinery of Government in War',
    6 June 1966.
12 Emergency Powers (Defence) Bill Draft, 19 March 1963.
13 TNA, PRO, CAB 175/28.
14 *Ibid.*
15 TNA, PRO, DEFE 10/402. Dr Edgar Anstey of JIGSAW (Joint Inter Services
    Group for the Study of All-Out War), 'Note on the Concept and Definitions of
    Breakdown', 10 June 1960.
16 Grant, *After the Bomb*.
17 Hansard, 21 February 1966.
18 *Ibid.*, 8 August 1966.

6

SPOTTING THE MUSHROOM CLOUDS

ACROSS EAST ANGLIA are well over 100 small underground bunkers. Most are in various states of disrepair, or lost beneath brambles and undergrowth. A few are preserved as reminders of a country under a horrifying threat. If nuclear war had broken out, it would have been volunteer members of the Royal Observer Corps (ROC) inside these cramped subterranean concrete boxes whose role would have been to warn their fellow citizens where Soviet nuclear bombs or missiles had fallen, and where nuclear fallout was spreading. Split from their families, confined in spartan surroundings, often in remote countryside areas, and knowing they might have to survive underground for a matter of weeks, and then only to emerge into a world with little or no future, theirs was not a job to be envied. Indeed, had the Cold War turned into conflict with unthinkable consequences, how many ROC members, working as the 'field force' of the UK Warning and Monitoring Organisation (UKWMO), would have abandoned their families, as they would have been required to do, and answered the call of duty for the sake of their neighbours? Thankfully, they were never put to that agonising test.

One volunteer, who served in Suffolk, recalls:

Had the call for 'transition to war' gone out how many would have turned up for duty? Certainly enough to ensure the warning and monitoring system worked. But there were some volunteers who said they would take a weapon into the bunker with them. Should the ultimate happen, a swift end might have been preferable to being left entombed facing a nuclear winter with little or no food or water.[1]

'I don't think anyone was convinced it would be survivable,' recalls another East Anglian volunteer, 'but there was a tremendous sense of duty regardless. After all, a slim chance is better than doing nothing and having no chance.' Another, commenting on whether survival was possible from a nuclear strike, said: 'For most, no. For some, yes. Our job was to help maximise the numbers who did survive.'[2]

Justyn Keeble, a member of the Royal Observer Corps Association Heritage Team, and a former Suffolk ROC volunteer, said: 'Very few of us were under any illusions. This was a job we had volunteered for and we didn't expect to survive in the long term. Our job was to try to save as many lives as we could under the direst of circumstances and thankfully we never had to find out how successful the system would or wouldn't have been.'

A survey of former ROC members, some twenty-two years after the ROC was disbanded, suggested that only two out of the fifty volunteers questioned would have failed to respond to the call to duty. A similar view is held by the former ROC Commandant of No. 6 Group, centred on Norwich. Harry Teague recalls:

> I could not be sure of a 100 per cent response, but I was sure that sufficient numbers would respond to bring the Group to operational readiness and stay at readiness. That, of course, meant that many of those who had responded to the transition to war call, including myself, would have had to leave their families. It would have been a dreadfully hard decision but volunteers knew what was at stake.[3]

It was often personal circumstances that would have imposed an unbearable strain on loyalties, had the call come. When asked if the pull to remain with one's family in such a terrifying situation would have been too hard to resist, one female Suffolk volunteer recalls that when she first joined the ROC she would have definitely answered the call. Then she had two children, and might have thought twice about it. When she had a third, disabled, child she knew she could not have abandoned her family, and resigned from the ROC.[4]

According to the historian of No. 6 Group Royal Observer Corps, from whose ranks the UKWMO drew the personnel whose daunting role would be to gather measurements of bomb bursts and radioactive fallout, some observers, who had signed up during the Second World War expecting to undertake the traditional ROC role of aircraft spotting and reporting, when informed in June 1955 of their new task in nuclear war, 'did not want to face the threat away from their families and resigned', but there were others to take their place.[5]

Volunteers anticipated having to remain several weeks in their primitive, claustrophobic and cold accommodation, but, like the crews who flew Britain's V-Force bombers, it was the aftermath of nuclear war that preyed on them. For bomber crews who survived their missions behind the Iron Curtain, it was uncertain whether there would be a base and a family in the UK to return to. For ROC members working for the UKWMO, should they emerge unscathed, it was whether life after the bomb would be worth their survival.

The UKWMO operated from 1955 until it was stood down in 1992. It was established under the aegis of the Home Office, but it was the uniformed volunteers from the ROC who staffed the bunkers and the Group Headquarters, where data from underground posts was processed by individuals trained to collate and interpret the information and issue warnings to the public.

As a government publication from the 1970s explained: 'The UK is very vulnerable to nuclear attack. But even if this happened, countless lives could still be saved – provided that the public was given even a few minutes' warning. Further large scale casualties could also be avoided if information on the pattern and path of any radioactive fallout could be gathered and broadcast quickly enough.'[6] The official line was designed to bolster public morale, but it was based on a well-planned system, and a substantial investment, that promised some protection for the public if the nuclear threat proved a reality. It was founded on Whitehall's belief that nuclear war would follow a period of rising international tension that would provide weeks or days in which 'transition to war' procedures, laid down in the *Government War Book*, could be implemented.

UKWMO planning apparently did not take into account the possibility of a Soviet 'out of the blue' first strike. A preventive initial strike by the USSR would have caught the UK entirely unprepared. It would have required up to seven days to gear up the whole warning and monitoring network, although Harry Teague recalls that, as a result of 'no-warning' call-out exercises, it proved possible to be virtually ready in a matter of five to ten hours.

However, the lesson from the 1962 Cuban Missile Crisis was that war could come unexpectedly. In October 1962, events moved rapidly and threateningly, but the Home Office took no steps to activate either Civil Defence or the UKWMO. This was despite the fact that Prime Minister Harold Macmillan had covertly ordered Bomber Command to an advanced state of alert. Within the RAF's V-Force, nuclear bombs were loaded and, for a time, crews waited in their cockpits five minutes from take-off.

The possibility of war came that close. But the vital link that might have helped protect the public was never activated.

UKWMO covered every square mile of East Anglia. Its bunkers, located approximately 8–10 miles apart, were organised into clusters of three to five, with one bunker acting as a master post. All the bunkers reported to a Group Headquarters.

Number 6 Group, which covered most of Norfolk and Suffolk, was one of twenty-five groups across the whole of the UK. The thirty-two bunkers serving 6 Group reported to a Group Headquarters bunker in Norwich, which was built in 1961 and became operational the following year. It was located at Chartwell Road, Old Catton. Three crews, each around thirty strong, were trained to man it but, had the chips been down, it would have needed forty-five to fifty observers to operate effectively.

Partly demolished in 2008, it was a three-level bunker. The top level was exposed and virtually unprotected, apart from a lack of windows and heavy blast-proof doors. The middle level was semi-sunken, by virtue of mounded earth banks, and the lower level was buried entirely below ground. It was equipped with its own standby services including water, sanitation, ventilation and decontamination facilities, as well as emergency food supplies. It was here that data would have been received from all the subterranean posts scattered across the group's area, then collated and plotted on a 'triangulation table'. Each nuclear burst, its location, height and size would have been displayed for the controllers to assess.

Information on areas threatened by radioactive fallout was monitored at five-minute intervals, so that up-to-date instructions could be provided to the public through broadcasted warnings. Data from the Norwich Group would also have been passed to neighbouring group control centres, the regional centre of government, local government control centres and, finally, to one of five sector controls.

Sector control for East Anglia was located at Lincoln, which doubled as both a group and a sector headquarters, and was staffed by around eighty trained personnel. The UKWMO was also linked to NATO, so that warnings of nuclear bursts striking countries in mainland Europe or Scandinavia could be received, together with predictions of the path and estimated time of arrival of any radioactive fallout swept by winds across the North Sea to East Anglia.

Other observation posts in East Anglia reported to Group Control centres at Colchester, Bedford or, as mentioned above, Lincoln. Like Norwich, two of these Group Controls, those at Bedford and Lincoln, were purpose-built and semi-sunken, affording some protection against blast damage and radioactive fallout. It is very doubtful they would have given much protection against a nuclear attack at town or city level. Colchester was even more vulnerable. It was also purpose-built, but sited on the surface with no underground protection. The decision whether to provide a semi-sunken or surface building was based on an assessment of how vulnerable the location was. Given that Colchester was a well-known garrison town, the choice of a surface building seems risky, but a former senior ROC member who worked at ROC Headquarters at Bentley Priory says: 'Barracks were most definitely not considered to be important or strategically worthy as targets. Warheads would have been aimed at active airbases, ports, communications centres, major cities and known locations of devolved government. Colchester would not rate highly enough in any USSR list to be considered a viable target'.[7]

Justyn Keeble was assigned to a bunker at Bacton in Suffolk, master post of a clutch of three in the Bury St Edmunds district, reporting to No. 4 Group Headquarters at Colchester. He recalls:

> The Control at Colchester was a tough building. If, however, it was knocked out our posts would reroute communications to another HQ. The control buildings should have survived a one megaton ground burst at 4 miles distance and it was anticipated there was not much difference between surface and semi-sunken control buildings on blast survival. Radioactive contamination could not enter the buildings because of the five to six psi overpressure when in lockdown mode.

Justyn was more concerned about the fact that two active airbases were within 10–12 miles of his bunker at Bacton: the V-bomber base at RAF Honington, and RAF Wattisham, an RAF fighter base and later the location for Bloodhound surface-to-air missile units.

At Norwich, in the early part of the Cold War, the RAF airfield at Horsham St Faith's would have been an obvious Soviet target. So, how safe was Group Control a short distance away across the city? Harry Teague says the main operations room was some 35ft below ground level:

> Of course nothing could give 100 per cent blast protection against even a small nuclear weapon detonated within a mile or so. At the height of the Cold War Norfolk could well have been devastated by a massive nuclear strike and not much would have survived it. The casualty rate might well have exceeded 95 per cent, but even with this dreadful figure there could well have been survivors who would need help and succour from whatever source in their efforts to survive.

The small underground bunkers which were the front line, the field force, of Britain's warning and monitoring system were built between 1957 and 1965 to a standard design. They were monolithic concrete structures, cast on location, buried and covered in earth. The 15ft-deep entrance shaft to each post was sealed with a steel hatch. Two ventilators, one part of the surface entrance to the bunker, the other at the far end of the underground chamber, were protected by either wooden or steel louvres. The idea was that the louvres would prevent fallout dust from entering the bunker, but some volunteers felt this was a vain hope. Provided the occupants were not so unfortunate to be close to ground zero of a nuclear strike, the bunkers should have given their three occupants a reasonable chance of survival. Blast waves from a nuclear explosion would pass over the top of the structure, and the surrounding earth and concrete would afford protection from radiation. That was the theory.

Instruments to plot and measure the size of nuclear explosions and to track the path and strength of radioactive fallout took the required measurements at the surface, while the readings were taken in relative safety down below. Radiation at the surface was captured by a fixed survey unit connected via a telescopic rod to an ionisation chamber of very strong rubberised plastic. This ensured that accurate measurements of roentgens per hour could be read on an indicator unit safely down below. A Radiac Survey Meter (RSM) was often used as a back-up, but it required readings to be taken outside the post, which would not have been a popular task. The observers were also issued with a personal dosimeter about the size of a fountain pen to detect the accumulated radiation the individual had been exposed to. The idea was to make sure no one exceeded a safe dosage in a given timeframe.

The position and height of a nuclear burst was determined by the Ground Zero Indicator (GZI). The device took the form of a cylindrical metal cover, beneath which were four concave faces each holding a piece of photographic paper in a cassette. Each of the faces was aligned with a small hole in the outer metal casing and lined up to match the four cardinal points of the compass – in effect, four pinhole cameras. When the intense glare of a nuclear burst entered the pinhole, the paper was exposed and the bearing and elevation of these spots could be accurately read off and recorded. The photographic papers needed to be changed at regular intervals, and it was the No. 3 Observer's task to do this either at predetermined times, when directed to do so by Group Control, or, in a war situation, one minute after the detection of a nuclear burst. The readings from a number of posts were triangulated at Group Control to work out the exact position of the nuclear explosion.

Changing the photographic paper on the GZI presented a real danger to the observer from fallout. Added to that was the possibility of bringing radiation back into the monitoring post. However, a well-trained observer could complete the task in under a minute.

The power of the burst was measured by a third device called the 'Bomb Power Indicator' which determined the peak pressure as the blast wave swept over the observation post. This reading could be used by Group Control, together with the distance from ground zero, to determine the power of the bomb or missile. Above ground, the instrument took the shape of a circular enamelled casing containing a bellows, which moved a pointer on a dial in the bunker when normal atmospheric pressure was exceeded by the pressure outside the post.[8]

Isolation, fear of the terrifying and unknown consequences of what was happening above them, the uncomfortably confined conditions, and a rapidly diminishing stock of food and water would have made the task of the three-person crews (often of mixed sex) difficult to bear. The allocation for each post was ten observers of either sex. A post should, therefore, have been able to call on up to two relief crews, but it was very uncertain how it would be possible to arrange a crew change following an attack. Harry Teague, Group Commandant for No. 6 Group, says: 'I always felt that the first crew on duty at each underground bunker would have to carry the job through.' The ROC volunteers were bolstered by a tremendous comradery and many trained and served for years during the Cold War decades. Harry Teague was in the corps 1950–89, while still working in his full-time job as a research chemist.

Given that crews might have had to stay down below for up to three weeks or more, the living conditions were rudimentary. The main working chamber, measuring 7ft by 16ft and 7ft high, was fitted with a two-tier steel-framed bunk bed, canvas chairs, a folding table and a store cupboard. There was little to insulate the bunker from cold, and some were unfortunate enough to become flooded, so a drainage sump was built into the floor to allow water to drain in and be pumped out with a rotary hand pump. A tiny adjunct to the main room held an Elsan chemical toilet, but once a nuclear attack had occurred the opportunities to empty it would have been minimal. Lighting was provided below ground by a single bulb or a fluorescent tube powered by a 12-volt car battery, periodically recharged by a petrol-driven charger. The only food available, apart from any brought in by the volunteers themselves, was in the shape of military ration packs, and even these were of limited use since the risk of fire or carbon dioxide poisoning would have severely reduced the chance of heating food or making a hot drink. Each post had a store of between four and six jerry cans of fresh water – although how 'fresh' it was depended on how frequently the crew replenished it, given that many bunkers were in fairly remote parts of the countryside.

The comparative isolation of some bunkers situated on farmland caused unexpected problems. In April 1961, a report from one Norfolk post to Group Headquarters stated: 'We wish to draw your attention to the fact that the Bomb Power Indicator tube [one of the devices protruding above the ground level] has been damaged by the landowner during ploughing.' Another report complained that 'due to livestock in the field it is impractical to get a vehicle within 300 yards of the post'.[9] Such were the problems of Britain's vital nuclear warning and monitoring organisation in rural areas.

Bunkers would be 'locked down' under fallout conditions, but periodically an air change was needed. A team at Group Headquarters had the task of monitoring the fallout plumes across their area and advising bunker crews when it was safe to open their hatches and vents to replenish the air inside the confined space within the bunker. Justyn Keeble recalls:

> An air change while fallout was dropping or wind was disturbing any ground dust containing radiation, would have been a problem, but as long as the contaminated ground cover was stable an air change would have been OK as the active particles would not be sucked down the entrance shaft. The master post was responsible for ensuring only one post in the cluster was under air replenishment in a given period. From our point of view at Bacton, RAF Wattisham was our nearest threat, and even if a one megaton device had been detonated, we would be pretty safe at ten miles distance. Being in East Anglia the entire place would've been rendered uninhabitable given the number of targets, and fresh drinking water would've been near impossible to find let alone food supplies, so our ultimate chances of survival would have been very low.

In most cases the only method of communication was by telephone landline, not a fail-proof method when the electromagnetic pulse of ionising radiation released by a nuclear explosion could cause major disruption to communications systems. Each bunker within a cluster was linked to the master bunker by landline. Only the master bunker was supplied with a radio to provide an alternative communications link to Group Headquarters if the landline failed. Master posts were also responsible for providing meteorological data and were equipped with an analogue display anemometer to record wind speed, crucial information required by the scientists at Group Control to calculate the spread of fallout and its future footprint.

Justyn Keeble recalls that his post was expected to function for a fortnight, and food and water would be taken into the post during the transition to war phase:

> These were standard military rations, but would also be supplemented with foodstuffs brought in by the Observers themselves. Along with personal kit it was initially advised that one day's worth of food be brought in by each Observer, however this was revised to two days by the 1980s. Power would be provided by a generator as long as fuel supplies lasted. Naturally all food and water would be strictly rationed.

The problem of accommodating, feeding and, particularly, providing sufficient water supplies for the fifty or so personnel based at Group Headquarters for a protracted period under nuclear attack was a particular concern for the Group Commandant. Harry Teague recalls:

> We always assumed we would be down in the 'hole' for several weeks. Control would have been provisioned with ration packs provided during the pre-attack phase. We had a large water tank, but water would be a major problem and next to security my chief headache. There would have been a constant demand for water and it would have had to have been rationed. After a few weeks we would have been a pretty dirty and smelly lot, but so would be the observers in their monitoring posts. Accommodation at Group Headquarters was less of a problem. We had two dormitories of bunks – even in the aftermath of a nuclear attack, males and females were kept apart – and volunteers would have had to accept 'hot-bedding', sharing bunks on a shift system.

Harry Teague was rightly worried about the security of his Group Headquarters bunker should nuclear war be imminent. It was located just off the city's ring road, close to housing areas, and was capable of accommodating some 200 people. How was he supposed to keep out terrified members of the public desperate to find some place to shelter from an imminent nuclear attack? 'I was never given any sensible advice from superior officers,' Harry says. 'We had a wire netting security fence and a couple of padlocks. What good was that against a determined mob fighting for their lives?'

The bunker network was also a crucial part of the means of warning the East Anglian population of imminent nuclear attack; what became recognised in the Cold War as the iconic 'four-minute warning'. From 1963 when RAF Fylingdales'

Ballistic Missile Early Warning System (BMEWS) became operational, the initial attack alarm would have emanated either from there, from NATO's early warning systems, or from a master radar station like RAF Neatishead in Norfolk. Passed to the Air Defence Operations Centre at Bentley Priory, it would have been transmitted immediately via what was codenamed the 'Handel Network'.

On the turn of a key the warning would be flashed to the BBC, and to 250 carrier control points across the UK, based at major police stations. At each of these points, which in East Anglia included places like King's Lynn, Norwich, Great Yarmouth, Bury St Edmunds, Ipswich, Colchester, Cambridge and Chelmsford, the simple step of pressing a button would have activated some 7,000 sirens across the UK, mostly in urban areas. They, in turn, were backed by around 11,000 other warning points in rural areas at police and fire stations, civil and military establishments, hospitals, industrial centres and ROC monitoring posts. Some of these warning points were in shops, pubs and private houses. Each was fitted with a battery-powered receiver that gave a spoken warning. Immediately that warning was received over the loudspeaker carrier network, the alarm would have been sounded using hand-operated sirens. In some rural parts of East Anglia the spoken warning would have been received by shopkeepers, publicans, even the local vicar, postmaster or bobby.

At the same time, warnings would be broadcast via television and radio. As a 1970s UKWMO leaflet claimed: 'It is estimated that the vast majority of the population would be alerted in time to take action to protect themselves against the danger.'[10]

However, what rudimentary protection they could have sought in their own homes was a question that those who lived through the Cold War years might well have been asking. There was no public shelter provision, as there had been in the Second World War. The government could not afford the immense sums it would have taken to build adequate shelters. The advice provided in the 'Protect & Survive' leaflets distributed to householders was almost laughably simple. 'Refuge rooms', which people were told to construct, would have taken time to build and equip, and were of questionable value anyway given the appalling threats from blast, heat and fallout.

Harry Teague says senior ROC officers were assured by the Home Office that at the proper time information and advice as to how to construct rudimentary protection in the home would be sent or broadcast to all households, via updated leaflets and constant radio broadcasts. 'Would the public have taken any notice? Probably not', is his comment looking back. 'When I first saw "Protect & Survive" leaflets and films at the Home Office Civil Defence School at Easingwold in Yorkshire they were the subject of much mirth and black humour.'

The ROC had the responsibility for issuing three types of warning: 'Attack Warning Red' was sounded by a siren using a wailing, rise and fall note, familiar from the days of the Blitz in the Second World War; 'Fallout Warning Black' was delivered by maroon, gong or whistle (three blasts in quick succession); while the 'All Clear' was sounded by siren on a steady note. To quote the UKWMO leaflet again: 'Through the existence, readiness and prompt response of UKWMO, ten million lives may have been saved – to see the dawn of another day.'[11]

The Royal Observer Corps had a proud history and a strong ethos of teamwork. As one writer put it, 'Members knew they had to depend on each other, so there was a tremendous amount of trust involved.'[12] The general public knew little of what was demanded of this largely volunteer body of men and women. 'It is not an organisation that is well known', wrote the historian of No. 6 Group, Brian Watson. 'Its work comes as a surprise to many people, but it makes a quiet contribution in service to Great Britain.'[13]

So why did government not widely publicise the UKWMO? Probably out of fear of alarming the general public. 'This question has puzzled me for years,' says Harry Teague. 'I can only surmise that the government was paranoid about panicking the population over the possibility of nuclear attack and the effect it would have had on public morale.'

NOTES

1 Information from Justyn Keeble, ROC Association Heritage Team, July 2013.
2 *Ibid.*
3 Correspondence with Harry Teague MBE, former group commandant, ROC Group 6, July 2013.
4 Information from Justyn Keeble.
5 Watson, Brian, *Some Kind of Club: The History of ROC Group Six* (Norfolk: No. 6 Group ROC, 1984).
6 'Protecting by Warning', UKWMO Official Publication, Home Office, 1979.
7 Information from Justyn Keeble.
8 Dalton, Mark, *The Royal Observer Corps Underground Monitoring Posts* (Bradford on Avon: Folly Books, 2011).
9 Watson, *Some Kind of Club.*
10 'Protecting by Warning'
11 *Ibid.*
12 Watson, *Some Kind of Club*
13 *Ibid.*

7

GERM WAR 'GUINEA PIGS'

THE COLD WAR posed many moral issues. When the population is under the threat of nuclear conflict, or the horrors of attack by chemical or biological weapons, ethics are not necessarily a government's first consideration. Nevertheless, some serious ethical issues surrounded a series of biological and chemical warfare experiments carried out in Norfolk by the Chemical Defence Experimental Establishment, based at Porton Down in Wiltshire, during the 1950s and 1960s. These were experiments undertaken in the deepest secrecy, using supposedly harmless substances which mimicked the physical properties of real chemical/biological warfare agents. The tests were designed to help the Ministry of Defence assess Britain's vulnerability if the Russians were to have released clouds of deadly germs over the country.

The notorious attack carried out by Saddam Hussein on some of his own population in the Kurdish town of Halabja, and more recently the use of chemical weapons in Syria, are brutal examples of how chemical and biological warfare is perhaps the most feared method of war ever inflicted on a civilian population. The First World War exposed the sheer horror that chemical agents could produce. In total 90,000 soldiers on all sides died agonising, choking deaths from the use of mustard gas, chlorine and phosgene on the battlefield, and up to 1.3 million were blinded or burned by the same agents. Modern chemical and biological weapons are even deadlier.

So, should the populations of Norwich and a large part of Norfolk be worried that, in 1964, they were made unsuspecting 'guinea pigs' in a simulated germ warfare attack? At least two sites in East Anglia were used in the 1940s for the manufacture and storage of poison gas for use in war, and for charging the bombs and spray weapons to deliver it. They were the forward filling depots at Barnham in Suffolk and Little Heath, Cambridgeshire operated by Nos 94 and 95 RAF Maintenance Units. But it took the Cold War to convince government scientists that realistic experiments in germ warfare should be carried out on unsuspecting populations.

While it was felt necessary for government scientists to conduct these experiments, the record of the Cold War shows they never led to any planned protection for the British population against the possibility of hostile biological or chemical attack. The armed services were provided with protective clothing and masks; military and government bunkers and control centres were equipped with filtration and 'scrubbing' devices to filter out the lethal elements and ensure survival; but the general population, unlike in the Second World War, were issued with no protection against such attacks, had the Soviet Union decided to use these horrific weapons. Certainly, the Russians contemplated doing so; they even defied international treaties, which they had signed, to step up production of chemical and biological agents. It is now clear that they continued manufacturing these ghastly products until after the fall of the Berlin wall.

From the mid-1950s both East and West were producing a raft of fast-acting, odourless agents that required minimum exposure in order to cause major trauma and death, without the wholesale destruction of buildings and facilities that would accompany nuclear conflict. As far back as July 1945, the British Chiefs of Staffs' conclusions on the Tizard Report, which foresaw the need for the UK to develop nuclear weapons, stated: 'Although biological weapons have not yet been used in war, we consider that the number of atomic weapons required would be materially reduced if biological weapons were simultaneously used.'[1] So, even in Britain, the concept of germ warfare was being discussed in secret meetings in Whitehall, eight years before the UK produced its own atomic bomb.

Nerve agents were the most potent development. Just one droplet on the skin could kill within a minute. Blister agents, too, had horrendous effects; so did germ warfare. To counter all of these, protective clothing needed to be worn for long periods. Such equipment, in the form of NBC (nuclear, biological and chemical) suits were issued to the services. When Civil Defence was radically scaled back in 1968 the government chose not to keep the public informed about, or protected from, potential chemical and biological warfare.

Soviet facilities to manufacture deadly biological agents far outstripped those in either the United States or Britain. Long after negotiations to ban such weapons, indeed right up until the collapse of the Soviet Union, the Soviets continued manufacturing them. When the Berlin Wall fell, Russia had fourteen factories producing chemical and biological agents and, after years of denial, Boris Yeltsin announced in 1992 that it possessed at least 50,000 tonnes for what he called 'defence' purposes. The British Government considered this a gross underestimate and thought the actual figure could be seven times that amount.

Vladimir Pasechnik, a senior Russian scientist who had been working on biological weapons, defected to Britain in October 1989. The secrets he disclosed to British Intelligence were horrific. He said that the Soviets had put great efforts into perfecting pneumonic plague as a weapon of war, using it in warheads. They were producing the plague agent on an industrial scale.[2]

Christopher Davis, who served on the British Defence Intelligence staff as the senior specialist on biological weapons and was one of those debriefing Pasechnik, said:

You choose plague because you're going to take out the other person's country. Full stop. That's what it is about. Plague is highly transmissible. Remember, one third of the population of Europe disappeared in the 13th Century with plague. And it's quick. If you don't get treatment within 12–24 hours at best, after symptoms appear in pneumonic plague you will die whether we give you antibiotics or not. It's over.[3]

The Biological and Toxin Weapons Convention was signed by the United States, the Soviet Union and the UK in 1972, but the Soviets had no intention of keeping their word. Indeed, they expanded their research using a concealed network of laboratories and institutes posing as civilian industrial facilities.

Soviet scientists conducted their massive programme under a series of codes. Bacteria such as plague, anthrax and brucellosis were bracketed under the prefix 'L', accompanied by an identifying number. Viruses like smallpox, Ebola and Marburg were given the prefix 'N' plus a number. Priority was given, under the codename 'Factor', to boosting the virulence factor of the strains that were being developed. 'Bonfire' was the code for a separate study to create a new generation of germs that would be totally resistant to antibiotics. Another line of research, codenamed 'Flute', was even more horrific – it was focused on manufacturing mind-altering compounds, in the search for a weapon that could make troops go crazy on the battlefield. Chemical weapons were worked on under a programme identified by the code 'Foliant' and, in other laboratories, scientists perfected germs to directly attack the West's agri-culture – weapons that could kill or wither food crops, or devastate livestock.[4]

The treaty prohibiting biological weapons was signed in London, Washington and Moscow in April 1972. The four-page document banned the production and development of biological weapons and the means of delivering them. However, there was a singular weakness. It lacked any agreement for onsite inspection because the Soviet Union refused to accept any verification clause. The West did not discover the full extent of the wide-scale deception the Russians had practised until the late 1980s – in fact, after the fall of the Berlin Wall. In 1992 when the British Foreign Secretary, Douglas Hurd, confronted Yeltsin about the Soviet biological weapons programme, the Russian president told him:

> It's still going ahead, even though the organisers claim it is merely defen-sive research. They are fanatics and they will not stop voluntarily. I know those people personally. I know their names and I know the addresses of the institutes where they are doing their work. I am going to close down the institutes, retire the director of the programme, and set the others to work designing something useful, such as a cow with a yearly yield of 10,000 litres! When I have checked for myself that the institutes have in fact stopped work, I'm going to ask for international inspection.[5]

Subsequently, American and British inspectors found that the Soviet pro-gramme had existed from 1946 right up to March of 1992. Even now, it is not known how far the Soviet Union went in creating warheads and bombs packed with the bacteria and viruses they had developed, or whether they had succeeded in producing a superplague resistant to antibiotics.

Among the communities in the UK secretly selected to be human 'guinea pigs' in chemical and biological attack simulations were the populations of Norwich and Norfolk. In a series of experiments in 1963 and 1964 a large area of Norfolk, and in particular the city of Norwich, was sprayed from the air as part of a meticulously planned operation to reproduce the exact condi-tions of a lethal biological attack.

A letter from the government's chief scientist to the Secretary of State for Defence, headed 'Secret, covering Top Secret' and dated May 1963, refers to the chemical and biological field trials to which Norwich and Norfolk were subjected.[6] 'At the Army Council meeting on 9 May 1963, when the annual report of your Scientific Advisory Council was discussed, you asked to be kept informed of all biological trials undertaken outside the confines of the War Department establishments,' the letter stated. With the letter was a brief report referring to the Norwich trials. 'I am convinced of the vital need for these trials which impose no hazard to the public,' the chief scientist wrote, 'although clearly, knowledge of them by unauthorised persons could be politically embarrassing'. It was nearly forty years before any official confirmation was released on exactly what took place.

The report sent to the Secretary of State said that trials performed in the years 1959–63, with the concurrence of the Offensive Evaluation Committee of the Chemical Defence Advisory Board, had shown that aircraft flying at night, or indeed ships or submarines offshore, were capable of disseminating biological agents which, under favourable weather conditions, could disseminate across wide areas of the UK. However, these experiments had not provided sufficient information on the concentrations likely to be reached in large urban areas.

Trials over Salisbury, the closest large urban area to Porton Down, had proved inconclusive due to local topographical conditions. 'Therefore trials are to be carried out in Norwich where the local conditions are more suitable.' The report made it clear that full co-operation had been covertly sought from the Meteorological Office, Home Office and Norwich City Police, and that the cover story for the operation, if difficult questions were asked, was that these were tests to measure 'air pollution'. Arrangements had been made for about six trials in which fluorescent particles of zinc cadmium sulphide would be disseminated from an aircraft flying on a course about 20 miles from Norwich.[7]

The Norwich experiments were not the first that the government had covertly undertaken. In March 1958, as a prelude to later wide-scale tests, a trial was conducted using a Valetta aircraft to establish whether it was possible to simulate a biological attack from the air. The later Norwich series of trials used a different aircraft, a Devon, spraying the biological warfare simulant at a rate of 2–3lbs of chemical per mile.

But before the experiments were launched on an unknowing public, Porton Down carried out a series of different operations. They were anxious to see if an undercover Russian spy could implement a devastating attack in Whitehall, and what the consequences would be. In the event, they were refused permission to use any of the government's buildings in the heart of Whitehall. Instead they chose to use the highly classified British Museum Art Repository in Westwood Quarry, Wiltshire – one of the deep storage bunkers where the nation's art treasures would have been taken for safe-keeping in the event of nuclear war. The scientists released live bacteria of the strain *Serratia marcescens*. Unfortunately the experiment went wrong. Quantities of the bacteria escaped and filtered into the adjoining Royal Enfield underground factory. At the time it was occupied by about 200 workers, none of whom had been warned by Porton Down of the experiment they were conducting next door. Because of the secrecy of the operation there was no subsequent monitoring of the health of the factory workers who may have been affected.

The UK was not alone in conducting germ war tests. Between 1949 and 1969 the United States carried out 239 open air trials. Several American cities were covertly used, like Norwich, as laboratories to test aerosols and dispersal methods. The locations were chosen because they had similar climate, urban and industrial development and topography as Soviet cities on a target list. The weapon used was a cluster bomb holding 536 biological 'bomblets'.

Much more realistic trials, using live agents, were undertaken by the US military at sea in 1965 and 1968. The 1968 experiments showed that a single airborne dissemination could disperse a virulent infectious agent effectively over nearly 1,000 square miles. British tests between 1963 and 1968 showed that, if released by a ship or an aircraft along a 100-mile-long line, significant concentrations of bacterial aerosol would gravitate more than 50 miles inland after a few hours. The trials confirmed that aerosolised bacteria could remain viable for several hours in the open, with 80 per cent of the population infected within 40 miles and half the population infected between 40–80 miles inland. These were truly doomsday weapons with hideous consequences.[8]

In the mid-fifties in Britain another series of experiments took place to simulate a sabotage operation. In this case, it was to examine the possibility of carriages being sprayed with a biological agent as a train passed through the confined area of a tunnel on the line between Salisbury and Exeter. Once again there was no warning to passengers that they were taking part in a germ war experiment. In 1956, bacteria was released on the London Underground, at lunchtime along the Northern Line, in an early simulation of the kind of terrorist attack that so concerns the authorities today. It was discovered that the organism dispersed widely and, in the case of the most deadly bacterial agents, only very small quantities would cause mass deaths.

The Norwich trials were regarded by the Porton Down scientists as essential to help the Ministry of Defence assess Britain's vulnerability if the Russians were to release clouds of deadly germs over the country, as they were certainly capable of doing. The agent sprayed above Norwich and the

Norfolk countryside was zinc cadmium sulphide, a chemical whose fluorescence allowed the spread to be monitored. While the government insisted the chemical was safe, cadmium is recognised as a cause of lung cancer, and during the Second World War, when used in high doses, it was considered by the Allies as a possible chemical weapon.

In 2000 the government declassified the comprehensive planning paper on the Norwich experiments (tagged 'Project 33'), written by top germ warfare scientists and published by the Superintendent Munitions Research Division of the Chemical Defence Experimental Establishment (CDEE), Porton Down. In great detail it outlines the parameters of the experiment which, from an administrative point of view, was based on RAF Swanton Morley where all the scientists from Porton Down were to be billeted. It explains why Norwich was chosen as a 'guinea pig' city:

> When an aerosol is generated in the atmosphere above a temperature inversion, it diffuses downward only slowly, and at night-time therefore it may drift over a wide area without penetrating to the ground to an appreciable extent. It has been suggested however, that in the vicinity of a large town the inversion is destroyed by the heat emitted from factory furnaces, domestic heating appliances, etc., and that sufficient turbulence is set up for aerosol material to be brought to ground level in larger concentrations than in the open country far outside the town.[9]

Attempts had been made to prove this hypothesis with trials at Salisbury, but the results had proved inconclusive because of the relatively small size of the urban area and the unevenness of the surrounding countryside. Norwich had been chosen because it was a larger conurbation, had more powerful heat sources and was in an area free from 'topographical irregularities'.

The paper describing the experiment says that the silicone-treated FP (fluorescent particles) would be 'quite innocuous' in the concentrations that would filter through to ground level and the cloud would diffuse so that 'members of the public will be oblivious of its presence'. The material would be released 400ft above ground level.

In Norwich, sampling was to take place at up to thirty positions in four groups based on Kett's Hill, with fifteen roadside positions. At all these points special filters mounted on 5ft-tall stakes would suck in air and record measurements of the presence of the chemical. At four police section boxes inside the city a more complex 'drum impactor' filter was to be installed to take regular readings of airborne particles.

The whole exercise was planned with military precision, and in Norwich revolved around a control point set up at police headquarters in the City Hall from where, via an aerial on the roof, constant contact could be maintained with the crew of the aircraft during its five-hour flight spreading its simulated 'deadly' load. Parked at the police HQ at City Hall was a monitoring unit, able to continuously sample the atmosphere to confirm the presence of FP. Wind and temperature profiles from ground level up to 1,000ft were monitored at various points, both inside and outside the city, using meteorological balloons sent up to intervals between 250ft and 1,000ft.

The briefing note placed emphasis on one significant point – Porton Down staff, it insisted, should be at all times 'incognito'. Their clothing, overalls and coats should, on no account, bear any lettering that might give the public the slightest hint that they came from the Chemical Defence Experimental Establishment at Porton Down.

In April 2000, when papers on the Porton Down Cold War era germ warfare trials were first declassified, and questions were asked in Parliament, DERA, the agency of the Ministry of Defence then responsible for the chemical and biological warfare facility at Porton Down, was asked for a full investigation into the zinc cadmium sulphide field trials, particularly in relation to any possible harmful medical effects on people who had been sprayed. The committee of scientists formed to undertake the research came up with the shocking conclusion that they could find no evidence that the toxicity of the chemical used had been examined at the time 'in any practical way by the Chemical Defence Experimental Establishment' before it was used on the public.[10] 'There is no "T" number for the compound: the absence of such a number tends to indicate that there was no formal toxicity testing at CDEE. There are no records in the archives of the former Medical Division of CDEE about FP toxicity testing or on its toxicity.'

However, the authors of the report examined some research conducted by the US National Research Council in 1997 which had been sponsored by the US Army. Quoting the US results, the report states: 'A small number of toxicity tests (which do not meet the current standards of toxicity testing) have suggested that it is not absorbed through the skin or gastrointestinal tract.' Having reviewed the US findings, the report goes on:

The subcommittee believes that the lack of solubility of ZnCdS [zinc cadmium sulphide] particles together with the limited toxicity studies implies that it will not be absorbed through the skin or gastrointestinal tract and that inhaled particles are not likely to be absorbed from the lung into blood for systemic distribution. Its lack of solubility also suggests that it is highly unlikely that free cadmium ions would become bio-available to target organs as a result of inhalation of ZnCdS. However, information is not available on whether ZnCdS might break down in the respiratory tract into more soluble components which could be easily absorbed into the body.

Looking in more detail at the US Army files, the British scientists said that the experiments carried out in America indicated that ZnCdS had negligible eye irritation problems. Dermal toxicity tests on rabbits had revealed no skin irritation, and oral tests on dogs and rats fed doses of the mixture released over Norwich suggested that ZnCdS was not 'acutely' toxic when swallowed in relatively small amounts. However, there had been no toxicity tests undertaken on the effect of inhalation of ZnCdS. How comforting all this might have been to anyone subjected to the germ warfare experiments forty years before is debateable.

In 2005, when the Cold War experiments were reported in the local and national press, the MP for Norwich South, Dr Ian Gibson, himself an experienced scientist, vigorously pursued the issue, and the *Norwich Evening News* reported that campaigners had claimed that the cadmium sprayed on the city in the mid-1960s could have doubled the number of oesophageal cancer cases in the Norwich area. They called for more studies.[11]

Mr Wyn Parry, a consultant at the Norfolk and Norwich University Hospital and a specialist in oesophageal cancer, told the Norwich evening newspaper: 'We don't know whether there is any link between cadmium and the number of cancers of the oesophagus. I see patients across Norfolk and we would expect to see between 120 and 130 cases (national average) but we are seeing between 170 and 180, perhaps 50 per cent more than the national population.'

The DERA committee concluded that:

Public knowledge would have led to much disquiet, even if the trials had been promulgated as essential meteorological research unconnected with biological warfare assessment and defence. During the period of the trials the Cold War was extant and the needs of defence security were paramount; there was no option beyond secrecy. Debate on the ethical aspect is unending. Whether such field trials use could be regarded as ethical or whether they violated the public trust through exposure to chemicals by the government without public knowledge or assent is not further examined in this report.[12]

The British scientists went on to say that it was quite clear that the US Army Chemical Corps and the UK authorities had accepted the view of the meteorological communities in both countries, that fluorescent particles posed no hazard to the exposed public, and this was the view originally propounded by Stanford University in California, which was the first to use FP in field trials. Nevertheless, the relevant operational manual cited the cadmium sulphide element of FP as of greater toxicity than the zinc sulphide element, and this had been based on toxicological data on cadmium sulphide from industrial concerns in the cadmium industry. They advised that it was good practice to store and handle FP as a potentially toxic material. However, the scientists confidently and reassuringly concluded that FP aerosol experiments 'may be run hundreds of times over the same populated area without subjecting any inhabitant to more than one millionth of the proven safe dosage; and the potentially toxic effects of any surface deposition of FP material produced by experimental operations are nil'.

In 2000, the Ministry of Defence refused to rule out undertaking further large-scale trials if necessary in future:

> In the event of a military question arising which could only be answered by conducting open air trials in areas which may involve the general public, Ministers have made it clear that they cannot rule out the need to conduct larger scale trials in the future to try to ensure the protection of the UK from attacks by peoples of states using biological or chemical weapons.[13]

In 2002, Porton Down reiterated that message. Sue Ellison, spokeswoman for the defence establishment, said that the results from the Cold War trials would save lives should the country or UK forces face an attack by chemical or biological weapons.[14]

The UN Chemical Weapons Convention of 1993 sought the complete global elimination of chemical arsenals, but as was demonstrated so terrifyingly in 2013, it was a treaty that Syria had refused to sign.

Following the horrific use of gas in the First World War, the further use of chemical weapons was banned under the Geneva Gas Protocol of 1925, but when the Second World War threatened Europe again the UK Government decided to manufacture mustard gas as a deterrent, since Germany was almost certainly producing chemical weapons.

In 1941 it was proposed to build five forward filling depots. One was located at Barnham on the Norfolk/Suffolk border, another at Lord's Bridge in Cambridgeshire. Barnham had storage capacity, in three underground tanks, for 1,500 tonnes of mustard gas and facilities to decant the agent into bombs and spray tanks. Between 1953 and 1954 the storage 'pots' were emptied, all the mustard gas removed, and the area thoroughly decontaminated. But it was not until 1995 that the remains of the storage 'pots' were finally excavated and taken from the site.

In today's world, dominated not by the conflict of two opposing political creeds, but far more by the fear of terrorism, an understanding of the potentially uncontrollable effects of these horrific forms of attack and possible ways of protecting against them remains a priority of government.

NOTES

1 Chiefs of Staff conclusions and recommendations on revised Tizard Committee Report; Humphrey Wynn, *RAF Nuclear Deterrent Forces*, (London: HMSO, 1994), Appendix 1, p.556.
2 Alibek, Ken, with Stephen Handelman, *Biohazard: The Chilling True Story of the Largest Covert Biological Weapons Programme in the World* (New York: Random House, 1999).
3 Hoffman, David E., *The Dead Hand: Reagan, Gorbachev and the Untold Story of the Cold War Arms Race* (London: Icon Books, 2011), p.334.
4 *Ibid.*, pp. 101–02.
5 Braithwaite, Sir Rodric, *Across the Moscow River* (New Haven: Yale, 2002), pp.142–43.
6 Letter from government chief scientist to Secretary of State for Defence, 30 May 1963, Reference CS/7/3.
7 Porton Field Trial Report No. 610, 'The Penetration of Built-Up Areas by Aerosol at Night', Government Experimental Establishment, Porton Down, Wiltshire.
8 Hoffman, *The Dead Hand*, pp. 121–22.
9 Porton Field Trial Report No. 610
10 DERA/CBD/JP000322. 'Zinc Cadmium Sulphide (Fluorescent Particles) Field Trials Conducted by UK: 1953–1964', April 2000.
11 *Eastern Evening News*, Norwich, 14 October 2005.
12 DERA/CBD/JP000322. 'Zinc Cadmium Sulphide', April 2000.
13 *Ibid.*
14 *Observer*, 21 April 2002.

8

PEEPING INTO RUSSIA'S BACKYARD

SUFFICIENT WARNING WAS the key to survival, and the chance to retaliate before all was lost in the Cold War. The crucial four minutes offered by the Ballistic Missile Early Warning System (BMEWS), with its high-powered radars based in Greenland, Alaska and RAF Fylingdales on the North Yorkshire Moors, became legendary. But four minutes is a frighteningly short time, and the search to guarantee a safer margin of alert led to the West seeking a system that could peer deeper behind the Iron Curtain and detect a missile launch at the point of firing, rather than part way through its deadly journey towards a target in the United Kingdom, possibly East Anglia.

An early attempt at over-the-horizon (OHT) radar was christened Project 440-L. It involved transmitting a signal into the ionosphere, bouncing it down to a receiver thousands of miles away, and recording any disturbance caused by a ballistic missile in flight. Known as 'forward scatter', the system required three transmitters, two of them in the Far East, and ten receivers across Europe. One of these receiving stations was at the former Thor missile base at RAF Feltwell, in Norfolk, after the missile pads there had closed down.

The project began to be used in 1968, but as it came into service the scientists were formulating an even more ambitious system, Project 441-L. Project 441-L became the West's most ambitious Cold War scheme to pry deep into the territory of the Soviet Union and the Warsaw Pact countries. This complex, and rather mysterious, project was set up at Orford Ness on the Suffolk coast in the late 1960s and early 1970s. Codenamed 'Cobra Mist', it was a highly secret collaboration between the UK Ministry of Defence and the American Department of Defense. It was one of the most powerful, spectacular and large-scale pieces of electronics ever seen in the UK.

Its location was appropriate. Some of the earliest work on the development of radar before the Second World War had taken place at Orford Ness, before being moved to Bawdsey Manor, a short distance away, where the work of Sir Robert Watson-Watt became crucial to Britain's survival in the Second World War.

In August 1967 the British Government issued an intentionally misleading press statement, inferring that what was planned on a part of Orford Ness, at the time still a trials and testing site for the Atomic Weapons Research Establishment, was a radio research station from which to conduct joint research into long-range propagation of radio signals. The same cover story had been used when the Feltwell project was announced. It was far from the whole truth.[1] The real purpose of the project, in this remote and secure part of East Anglia, was to project radar far into the USSR and its satellite countries. The object was to beam signals up to the ionosphere, and reflect them over the horizon to monitor air and missile activity at extreme range.

Declassified documents, released by the Pentagon over a quarter of a century later as a result of Freedom of Information Act (FOIA) requests, reveal that speculation at the time about the installation's real purpose was broadly correct.[2] The radar bounced its signals off the ionosphere and listened for the return pulse along the same path. 'The missions of back-scatter radar', the Pentagon admitted, 'are to detect and track aircraft; detect missile and earth satellite vehicle launchings; fulfil current and critical intelligence requirements; and to provide a research and development test bed for determining optimum back-scatter techniques for other operational missions.' This detailed explanation made clear that the project at Orford Ness was designed to detect and track aircraft at ranges up to 2,000 nautical miles. The installation was capable of being switched to a 'searchlight' mode to enable high-priority targets, whose approximate locations were known in advance, to be homed in on. Such targets could be single aircraft, formations of aircraft or missile launches. Alternatively, the radar could be used in a 'scanning mode', which meant it could be used to search in maximum azimuth and range over any chosen sector of the radar coverage.

Originally 'Cobra Mist' was conceived to be built at Diyarbakir in Turkey, but concerns about the security there persuaded the Americans to seek a site in the UK. Final agreement to its construction in the UK was obtained from the Labour government in June 1967.

'Cobra Mist' was to be part of a series of 'Cobra' stations designed to scan Russian, and possibly also Chinese, missile tests. On Shemya Island at the end of the Aleutian Islands, just south of the Arctic Circle off Alaska, a huge aerial array, known as 'Cobra Dane', was built to monitor Russian missile warheads as they re-entered the atmosphere at the end of their test firings. A US ship, known as 'Observation Island', was stationed near the Kamchatka Peninsula, code named 'Cobra Judy'. Two modified RC-135 aircraft known as 'Cobra Ball', packed with long-range photographic and telemetry gear, flew out of Shemya Island, also keeping close checks on Soviet missile activity.

Orford Ness and 'Cobra Mist' were to complement the reach of the 'Cobra' network. One of the distinct attractions of Orford was that it enabled the Americans to spy on the Soviet Northern Fleet Missile Test Centre at Plesetsk. The centre of the fan array, with a bearing of about 60° north-west, appeared to be aligned directly at the Russians' missile test base. It was the strangest, and probably the most ambitious, of the whole 'Cobra' range.

The agreement between the US and UK governments provided for the Americans to supply and pay for the materials, and to foot the bill for the bulk of the running costs. The Americans also expressed a willingness to give the substantial associated construction contracts to British firms. Obviously this suited the British authorities, but there remained a serious concern on behalf of the British. They wanted a clause in the agreement that the enormous transmission power output would not have a damaging environmental impact, either out to sea where it could affect shipping, or in the airspace where it might interfere with aviation or communications.

The cost to the Americans was estimated at close to £55 million, but that figure was considerably inflated by the pioneering technology that meant constant changes in the plans and specifications. Subsequent estimates suggest the final figure grew to almost three times that amount.

The radar was officially known as AN/FPS-95 OTH (Over The Horizon) and its official code name – apart from Cobra Mist – was 'Sentinel Fan', appropriate because the massive aerial array that emerged looked very much like a vast fan. It was the most powerful and sophisticated back-scatter radar of its kind, emitting a peak power of 10 megawatts, and an average of 600 kilowatts.

Building work started in 1968, and many of the 150-strong labour force, bussed in to the remote site daily, were workers who had recently completed construction of Sizewell A, the Magnox nuclear power station a few miles along the coast to the north. Building continued round the clock, but, because of difficulties, delays and constant design modifications, the project began to fall seriously behind schedule. Much of the land was marsh, and it was necessary to drain off excess water, which required building new pumping stations. The threat of flood meant that flood barriers had to be installed, and the huge main control building needed to be raised on stilts 8ft above ground level to lift it clear of the flood height reached in the historic east coast floods of 1953.

The American military were getting impatient, but by September 1969 they had to accept that the whole timetable required drastic revision, and there was little possibility of reaching the point where trial operations could begin before 1972.

'Cobra Mist's' aerial was weird, and dominated the landscape. The huge fan-shaped spider's web of antennae covered 135 acres. It was highest on the landward side, and tilted down towards the sea. The masts that supported the array ranged from 42ft closest to the sea, to 180ft on the landward side. Between these masts were eighteen antenna strings radiating like the spokes of a wheel from a central hub. Each measured 1,800ft long, and together they formed a 119° sector of a circle. The antennae were connected to a harmonic filter bank intended to cut out background noise.

The final part of the project to be built was the 'blockhouse' – the control centre for the project. The building, even given its remote location, was highly secure. Enclosed in a steel frame, it had no windows and its triple steel wall protected it from any kind of electronic intelligence penetration. Cables connecting the aerial array and the blockhouse were housed in an underground switch chamber lined with copper. Externally, the whole 700-acre site was surrounded by 6ft fencing, plus a further 40-yard security cordon outside the main fence. Furthermore, the Orford Ness site could only be accessed from the mainland by boat or landing craft. Few places in East Anglia were more secure.

During 1970, with construction hitting delays, a further factor emerged which raised such serious concerns with the British Government that discussions reached Cabinet level. They focused on possible dangers created by the high levels of radiation emanating from the aerial. Should the government admit to these possible dangers? Would it undermine the cover story already in the public domain, that the project was an advanced radio transmission station, not an OTH surveillance radar?

The issue was particularly sensitive because, at the time that it surfaced, the opposing powers, East and West, were negotiating the Strategic Arms Limitations Treaties (SALT).

Locally, queries emerged as to possible interference with television signals. The authorities had to admit that some interference was a possibility, but more serious were the questions being raised on the impact of radiation on heart pacemakers and other human health issues. The Americans conducted research at Brooks Air Force Base in Texas, which concluded that, as the direction of most radiation would be out to sea, only mariners might be affected. Further research indicated that only one type of pacemaker might be at risk, and provided any local users fitted with this particular type were warned to keep clear of the area, no major threat should exist.

Nevertheless, the British Government felt it necessary to issue an official warning to aircraft that 'within a radius of 3 miles of the installation and up to an altitude of 6,000ft, there might be some radio interference which could cause damage to HF/MF receiving equipment, and there was a remote possibility of triggering the accidental operation of electrically initiated explosive charges'. The authorities issued a similar warning to mariners, that any interference within a defined area would be similar to that triggered by a normal electric storm. The matter was sensitive enough for the American Embassy to insist that any press statement issued by the British authorities should first be vetted by the Americans, who were adamant that any alarmist stories should be effectively suppressed before the British press could get hold of them.

A press release dated 26 February 1971 effectively played down the emerging fears. Entitled 'Research into long range radio propagation'[3] it stated:

> There is no question of any biological hazard outside the boundaries of the station. The remote possibility exists of occasional mild electrical side-effects in the near vicinity of the high-powered radio system. ... Though extremely unlikely to occur, the possible side effects are as follows: Mild and harmless electrical shocks from metal rigging or metal structures accompanied by slight sparking; damage to radio equipment if connected to an external aerial; and the spontaneous operation of certain kinds of electrically initiated devices which are normally carried only by commercial and military vessels and aircraft.

But if the 'Sir Humphreys' in Whitehall thought this would be an end of the matter, they were wrong. A few days later the *Observer* newspaper published an article headlined: 'It's getting a bit like *Doomwatch* around here!'[4] The report blew the cover of experiments in high-powered radio transmissions. It said local residents claimed the station was using 'over the horizon' methods to give better warning of any Soviet nuclear attack. And it added a comment by one resident: 'I don't think the scientists themselves know what the effects will be.'

All this aroused further media attention. In June, the *Daily Express* carried a report by its defence correspondent, Chapman Pincher, in which he argued that 'Cobra Mist' provided the Soviets with a strong reason for a retaliatory attack, and erroneously suggested that it would give the US military the capability to project surveillance across the whole of the USSR.[5] Pincher's other allegation, that it was contrary to treaty obligations under the SALT negotiations, was particularly provocative and led to mounting suspicions about the real intention of 'Cobra Mist'.

Further embarrassment was to come. In August 1972, both *The Times* and the *Daily Telegraph* followed up on an article in the respected US journal, *Aviation* Week,[6] which had described its true purpose as OTH radar. British newspaper reports quoted the *Aviation Week* disclosures, and again posed the question whether such an installation coming on stream at that particular point breached the SALT agreements.

A secret memorandum from the Ministry of Defence, dated 19 September 1972, admitted that there were serious difficulties in sustaining the cover story of long-range radio transmissions, in the face of newspaper reports and leaks in the US technical press. It also spoke of worrying problems of delays and even of making the system work effectively. The memo also accepted that suggestions of a conflict with the SALT commitments held some weight. The British Government – by this time a Conservative administration under Edward Heath – was already operating its own surveillance operations based in Cyprus and Hong Kong, and began questioning the need for 'Cobra Mist'.

However, the British military were still convinced of the station's potential. In November 1971 the undersecretary of state at the Ministry of Defence wrote, in an official memo, that if it could be made to work the project would be 'of inestimable value'.[7] But, despite this expression of confidence, there was growing acceptance in the Ministry of Defence that, while the science of the project was impeccable, the test transmissions were proving unacceptable. One classified report said, 'most of the problems appeared to be in the receiver and signal processing areas, since it was known that the transmitters were working and the antenna was radiating at expected power levels'.[8]

During the summer and autumn of 1972, severe background noise was polluting the signals received in the blockhouse at Orford Ness and this greatly reduced the ability of the operators to decipher and identify the targets they were seeking inside the Iron Curtain. Considerable efforts were made to establish the source of the noise in order to eliminate it. By the end of December 1972, it was agreed to form a joint US/UK team of eminent scientists and OTH radar specialists to try to determine the cause of the problem and to recommend a way forward. It is clear, from papers declassified some thirty years later, that the Cobra Mist Scientific Assessment Committee came up with a detailed analysis and some positive recommendations, but the truth was, the finest brains that the American and British scientific communities could gather could not come up with a definitive solution.[9] They ended their report with a poetic flourish, quoting from Shakespeare's *The Tempest*:

> This is as strange a maze as e'er men trod,
> And there is in this business more than nature
> Was ever conduct of: some oracle
> Must rectify our knowledge.

It amounted to a nail in the coffin for 'Cobra Mist'. The source of the noise, and a means to eliminate it, was never found. The two governments decided the economics of the situation were unjustified, and the project was terminated. On 19 June 1973 the UK was advised that the US Government had concluded the project should be closed down and the system deactivated. Ten days later funds were abruptly withdrawn, and some ninety local staff were sacked with a day's notice.

So, what put paid to such an expensive and ambitious Cold War project? One theory was that the wet nature of the marshy site might have caused corrosion, which in turn affected the giant aerial. Another suggested that the cause was the screening of the signals between transmitters and receivers within a single building, and that it might have been eliminated by basing transmission and reception on separate, widely spaced, sites. Or perhaps it just boiled down to the conclusion that 'Cobra Mist' was too ambitious to work as planned.

Another possibility could purely have been diplomatic. Was abandonment of the project, without throwing even more money at solving the problems, a means of gaining leverage in the ongoing talks between East and West on limiting strategic weapons? Certainly the Russians could not have been unaware of the powerful bursts of radio signals beamed across large swathes of their territory.

Was the project torpedoed by the success of satellite surveillance, which was becoming more and more accurate and reliable?

Finally, and perhaps more likely, was 'Cobra Mist' defeated by Soviet Union jamming? There is no doubt that the Russians were very efficient at jamming signals elsewhere in Cold War situations, and jamming could have produced the kind of effect that made the complex system so ineffective. Certainly the

Russians routinely sent so-called 'trawlers', bristling with aerials, to conduct surveillance and jamming off the coast of East Anglia and elsewhere around the British Isles.

Towards the end of the summer of 1971, when full power trials were proceeding, there were some 200 service personnel on the site; the majority were Americans who were accommodated at the nearby USAF base, RAF Bentwaters. An RAF presence of around forty-five was nominally attached to RAF Orford Ness but billeted at the nearby RAF Bawsey base. Additionally, there were still around 100 UK civilian technicians and operators employed by the Ministry of Defence and the Department of Public Building and Works, together with 150 contractors' employees. Naturally, there was consternation and anger when the closure was announced, because a large number of civilians were made redundant. Lord Carrington, Defence Secretary, had to deny that there had been any sort of conspiracy by the Americans at British expense. The local MP, Sir Harwood Harrison, expressed disgust given that there had been such urgency to get the project finished just three years previously.

Some idea of what it was like to work at 'Cobra Mist', and the remarkably high security that surrounded it, can be gauged from the recollections of one American serviceman who was there during the test trials.[10] Bob Rudasill, like all his American colleagues, had to go through a special form of security clearance in the United States before being posted to RAF Orford Ness. He describes the USAF Extended Background Investigation (EBI) as extraordinarily thorough. It must have been. It took a year before he was finally cleared and approved to deal with the highly classified information his job entailed. 'Cobra Mist' was run by the American 81st Radio Research Squadron of the USAF Security Service, reporting directly to the National Security Agency back in the States. 'My days would be spent', Rudasill recalls:

... dealing with the National Security Agency, the Defense Intelligence Agency and other intelligence organisations on a daily basis.

We were officially assigned to RAF Bentwaters for use of their facilities, and for security reasons we were instructed not to mention RAF Orford Ness. It soon became apparent that we needed a physical location and a squadron designation as a cover. That is when the 81st Radio Research Squadron [81st RRS] came into existence.

Clearly the cover story the two governments had used to disguise the real purpose of 'Cobra Mist' was adhered to, even in the designation of the unit to which those working at Orford were officially attached. Bob continues that the unit's administrative office, based at RAF Woodbridge, 2 miles from RAF Bentwaters (the two USAF flying bases were known locally as the twin bases), was little more than a 'front', but that is where they were told to say they worked. There was, he says, tremendous interest and speculation from the outside world about what was happening at Orford Ness. For most its exact purpose was shrouded in mystery.

His daily journey to work involved being taken by bus to Orford where, in order to gain access to the site, he and his colleagues' ID cards were checked prior to them all boarding a Second World War landing craft to take them across the River Ore to Orford Ness 'island'. In reality, Orford Ness was not an island at all but a spit of land jutting out into the North Sea, treeless and inhospitable, barely rising above sea level.

Once on the 'island' the USAF personnel boarded another bus to be driven 1 mile or so along a narrow road to the guard house. There, an armed guard would board the bus and again check all ID cards before allowing admittance to the site. 'We had what was known as a dual badge system,' he recounts. 'This consisted of an ID card with our picture and name. This card was handed over to the armed guard at the gate and he would issue us with a matching badge.'

Bob Rudasill gives no detail as to what his actual duties were, but says that he worked in the windowless three-storey control centre:

> Each floor of the building was represented by a colour. First floor blue, second red, and third green. Your badge would display the colours of the floors you were authorised to access. I was authorised for all floors, so my badge had three coloured squares. Inside the building there was a guard on each floor and cameras scanning every hallway and office.

He mentions that, in order to reach critical work areas, it was necessary to enter a cipher-locked door which opened into a room only big enough to accommodate two people at a time. Once inside, the door automatically shut and locked behind you. 'There was an armed guard sitting behind a bulletproof window who once again checked your ID prior to your entering through another cipher locked door which led to the Vault, the most secure room in the building. That was where my days were spent.'

Basically, the transmitter hall occupied the lower part of the building and the receiver hall was upstairs. Areas of the building were Faraday-screened, with special door seals of beryllium copper strip.

'When we left the building', he recalls, 'all work related conversations ended, but mentally you could not walk away from the situation. It is like someone telling you an ultimate secret and you can't tell anyone. Work related topics stayed on the island.'

When 'Cobra Mist' was suddenly closed down and the American personnel were told they would have to be transferred elsewhere, Bob and his colleagues found that there were only limited postings for people with such high security clearance. Bob was moved to RAF Croughton, a USAF communications unit in Northamptonshire which processed approximately a third of all military communications in the European area.

The huge 'Cobra Mist' antennae array was dismantled, and the complex transmitter and receiver equipment removed by the USAF for shipment back to the United States. The control building was offered to the BBC's Overseas Service as a replacement for its medium-wave transmission station at Crowborough, Sussex. A dozen broadcasting masts were erected, and in 1975 World Service broadcasts were commenced to eastern and central Europe, a strange twist on the former project to beam OTH radar towards much the same area.

'Cobra Mist' was a fact, but here we enter into the realms of myth or fantasy (or maybe not!). The declassified Pentagon report on the project, published thirty years later, acknowledges that 'Cobra Mist' 'is well known for its association with Unidentified Flying Objects [UFOs]'. It is an intriguing reference to find in a US government paper, relating to a strange happening in Rendlesham Forest, some 5 miles inland from Orford Ness, on Boxing Day night 1980. A few hundred metres from the end of the runway of the USAF base at Woodbridge, brilliant lights were seen amongst the trees, and subsequently, evidence was found of damage caused by what appeared to have been the crash of a large object. Exactly what occurred there has been surrounded by rumour and doubt ever since, and has entered the folklore of conspiracy and UFO theorists.

A number of American servicemen were said to have witnessed the aftermath of the incident, and the response of British and American authorities caused widespread suspicion that the facts were being suppressed. UFO enthusiasts claimed an alien spaceship had crashed or landed at Rendlesham. The deputy commander of RAF Bentwaters was instructed by the American authorities to make an official investigation. USAF personnel who were believed to have personally witnessed what happened were sent back to the States, and the actions of the authorities, both military and civilian, provoked further rumours and speculation.

One theory, which received wide publicity in a book written by Jenny Randles,[11] was that part of a Soviet 'Cosmos' satellite had crashed into

Rendlesham Forest that Boxing Day night. The theory suggested that the US National Security Agency had developed a successor to 'Cobra Mist', code named 'Cold Witness'. Its purpose, the story went, was to incapacitate and bring down a Soviet satellite – perhaps a precursor to Ronald Reagan's famous 1983 Strategic Defense Initiative (SDI). (Reagan announced the Strategic Defense Initiative Organisation in 1984 to oversee development of a programme headed by a past director of the NASA space shuttle programme.) Some credence was lent to this in April 1990, when the then defence minister, Alan Clark, admitted to Parliament that there was indeed a system code named 'Cold Witness', a successor to 'Cobra Mist'. He said that the project had been abandoned and asserted that it had never been operated from Great Britain, and certainly not from Orford Ness.[12]

However, there is some circumstantial evidence that the Ministry of Defence continued to operate a form of surveillance from the Orford Ness site following the demise of 'Cobra Mist'. But, if that was truly the case, it is still subject to security because no concrete proof has emerged.

There is perhaps one final intriguing clue. When the government released Ministry of Defence files on UFO sightings, in the summer of 2009, included among them was a statement by the former chairman of the NATO Military Committee and chief of the defence staff, Lord Hill-Norton, dated 1985, in which he said there was 'no case for denying any defence interest' in the Rendlesham incident; on the contrary it was of the 'utmost defence interest'!

NOTES

1 MOD Press Release, 24 August 1967.
2 Freedom of Information Act (FOIA), documents on 'The Cobra Mist (AN/FPS-95) Over the Horizon Radar', May 1993.
3 *Ibid.*
4 *Observer*, March 1971.
5 *Daily Express*, 1 June 1971.
6 *Aviation Week*, December 1971.
7 Ministry of Defence memorandum, 5 November 1971.
8 Ministry of Defence Report, 19 September 1972.
9 FOIA documents, May 1993.
10 'Life of Spy Guy', United States Air Force Security Service, http://bobrudasill.me/The_Life_of_Spy_Guy/Cobra_Mist.html
11 Randles, Jenny, *From Out of the Blue* (New Brunswick, New Jersey: Global Communications, 1991).
12 Debate in House of Commons, 23 April 1990, Hansard, Vol. 171 cc 63–73W.

9

'BROKEN ARROW'

IN 1979, REPORTS began circulating on both sides of the Atlantic regarding an alleged cover-up of a nuclear 'near disaster' that had happened, some twenty-three years earlier, at the giant American airbase at Lakenheath, in Suffolk. British and American newspapers quoted a retired USAF major general as saying that there had been a real threat to East Anglia of a horrific nuclear explosion. 'It is possible', he said,'that a part of Eastern England would have become a desert.'[1]

There is no doubt that what happened at Lakenheath, on that summer's day in late July 1956, was a significant nuclear emergency, significant enough to be classed among the handful of worst-case scenarios of nuclear accidents experienced during the Cold War, each codenamed 'Broken Arrow'. There is also no doubt that the USAF authorities and Washington, together with Anthony Eden's government in the UK, 'hushed up' the full story at the time, assisted by the fact that Downing Street and Whitehall had been plunged into the deeply controversial Suez Crisis only the day before. It is true that no official report was given by the British Government, until a statement by the Secretary of State for Defence, Mr Francis Pym, in November 1979.[2]

The incident involved a B-47 American bomber which lost control while landing at Lakenheath, sliding off the runway and crashing into a storage igloo which contained several Mark 6 nuclear bombs. Each Mark 6 had a yield ten times greater than that of the bomb that destroyed Hiroshima.

A telex from General Walsh, the commander of the 7th Air Division in England, to General Curtis Le May, Commander of America's Strategic Air Command, classified for many years as 'Top Secret', gives the horrifying details:

Have just come from wreckage of B-47 which ploughed into an igloo at Lakenheath. The B-47 tore apart the igloo and knocked about three Mark Sixes. Aircraft then exploded showering burning fuel over all. Crew perished. Most of the aircraft wreckage pivoted on igloo and came to rest with aircraft nose just beyond the igloo bank which kept main fuel fire outside smashed igloo. Preliminary exam by bomb disposal officer says a miracle that one Mark Six with exposed detonators didn't go off.[3]

As one USAF officer remarked: 'Near disaster was averted by tremendous heroism, good fortune and the will of God.' An observation underlined by the fact that, together, the three Mark 6 nuclear bombs stored in the Lakenheath igloo had the potential to produce an explosion greater than all of the bombs dropped in the Second World War.

The reaction on base was instructive. Some reports at the time commented on 'not just panic but a stampede out of Lakenheath'. Witnesses included the British civilian divisional fire officer from nearby Bury St Edmunds. Suffolk Fire Service was called to the base to provide a standby service for the US crews who were dealing with the crash. As they travelled towards the base the fire brigade encountered 'a convoy of American cars full up with women and children. They were panicking and simply trying to get away. It was a pretty amazing sight …'[4]

A local garage and taxi proprietor recalled that, at Brandon, some 3–4 miles from the base, 'there was a stream of traffic through the town in the middle of the afternoon'. One USAF airman was said to have hailed a taxi with the instructions: 'Go anywhere – just get away from here.'

At Strategic Air Command bases like Lakenheath the nuclear bombs and their cores were kept in different bunkers, shielded by earthen berms and concrete walls 10ft thick. The bunkers were built near the runways by order of the US Joint Chiefs of Staff 'to provide rapid availability for use'. Undoubtedly for East Anglia, it was a miracle the B-47 crashed into the igloo containing the Mark 6 bombs and not their nuclear cores. Had it done so, the results could have been horrific.

An article published in the *Omaha World Herald*, Nebraska, the newspaper closest to the headquarters of America's Strategic Air Command, reported in June 1979 that the steel casing of the Mark 6 bomb was relatively thin and the resistance of the bomb to heat was not especially great. Each bomb contained a substantial amount of conventional TNT, which if it exploded would have produced a 'geyser of radioactive material'. The newspaper said that the fire chief at the base, Air Force Master Sergeant L.H. Dunn, who was riding in the lead truck, moved as close as possible to the building containing the bombs and poured flame-suppressing foam on the fire. He ignored the four B-47 crew members trapped inside the wreckage on the presumption that they were already dead, and used four foam trucks to extinguish the fire around the storage igloo. His efforts, and those of his crews, showed great heroism. Indeed, the commander of 7th Air Division, in his telex to General LeMay, noted that he was investigating whether their actions warranted bravery awards.

Did East Anglia face nuclear devastation on that summer day in July 1956? Well, the experts insist there was no question of anything so catastrophically serious. In their book, *Broken Arrow: The History of US Nuclear Weapons Accidents*, two former USAF nuclear specialists, Michael H. Maggelet and James C. Oskins, are adamant there was no such threat.[5] They tell the story of the flight taken from official Department of Defense records.[6]

The B-47 took off from Lakenheath at 9.35 a.m. for a scheduled six-hour combat crew training mission. The crew of four were on a routine temporary deployment to the UK from Lincoln Air Force Base in Nebraska. The object of the flight was to test the aircraft's radar system, accomplish an air refuelling rendezvous, and complete a series of pilot proficiency tests including practising instrument approaches and landings. The aircraft returned to Lakenheath at the end of its mission, where it was cleared by the base control tower to remain in the local area for a number of 'touch and go' landings. The B-47 made three such landings successfully, but on the fourth it veered off the runway, ending in the fatal crash into the nuclear weapons store.

The researchers, using their expert technical knowledge of nuclear weapons and explosive ordinance, and details now declassified by the Pentagon, say that even if the high explosive in the three nuclear bombs had exploded there was no possibility of a nuclear detonation or severe contamination. The bombs were stored without their nuclear cores, and the cores were not present in the igloo into which the aircraft crashed. Without a nuclear capsule the Mark 6 contained only natural uranium, and a one-point detonation would not have turned eastern England into any kind of wasteland.

Early American and British nuclear weapon designs kept the nuclear core separate from the weapon, making a true nuclear detonation impossible until the capsule was inserted. Early bombs did contain a quantity of natural uranium in the tamper but this could not pose a nuclear detonation hazard due to the extremely low level of radioactivity.[7] The implosion process used to detonate a nuclear device has a built-in safety feature. If the high explosive detonates for any reason, including fire or shock as a result of an accident, there would be no symmetrical implosion. The shockwave moving from a single point on the high-explosive surface would explode and destroy the weapon. This would release, and perhaps scatter, the active material but would not result in a nuclear explosion.

However, if the B-47 had struck a neighbouring igloo where the nuclear cores for the bombs were stored the story could have been very different. Had that igloo been torn open and set on fire, a cloud of plutonium could have floated across the Suffolk countryside, spreading radiation in its wake.[8]

The year after the Lakenheath incident, in 1957, the UK experienced its worst civilian nuclear incident when fire broke out at the Atomic Energy Authority's Windscale plant in Cumbria. The government remained tight-lipped about the alarming extent of radioactive fallout from the accident at Britain's first reactor. The prime minister at the time, Harold Macmillan, took steps to heavily censor the report into the fire. Behind the scenes, Whitehall asked Washington what the joint governments should do in the event of a nuclear accident occurring on an American airbase in the UK, or a US plane carrying nuclear weapons crashing in the UK. Washington replied that it already had a major contingency plan in place to prevent public panic, a strategy which had been tested after a non-nuclear accident in the States. London was not convinced.[9]

In Whitehall there was an awareness of the sensitivity, in some parts of the British public, over US bases in the UK. The British Government knew that the press in the UK would always ask if nuclear weapons were involved. It decided that Washington's freedom to talk to the press about any serious incident in the UK involving nuclear weapons should be curtailed. One memo, now declassified, states:

> It must clearly be for the British Government to provide the necessary background should a crash take place of an aircraft carrying a nuclear weapon. The Foreign Office has asked the Americans to ensure that in the event of such a crash, no press release is issued without prior consultation with the Ministry of Defence. It does not seem right that the US authorities should make statements about evacuated areas or about decontamination. I think it is certainly right that the Americans should be discouraged from making statements, particularly about evacuation.
>
> ... Any questions about nuclear weapons should be answered on the lines that a further statement will be made by the Air Ministry as soon as the facts are known.

By 1960, this policy had hardened to effectively denying everything until it was no longer plausible to maintain the line. In one Air Ministry document a civil servant describes what to do in various scenarios:

> Initial inquiries from the press should be answered with a factual statement that an aircraft of a named type crashed at a named location at a named time, together with any information about casualties which can be released under normal procedures. If at the time this statement is made a nuclear weapon is known to have been carried or the position is uncertain, any questions about nuclear weapons should be answered on the lines that a further statement will be made by the Air Ministry as soon as the facts are known. If it is known that no nuclear weapon was involved, the sooner this is stated the better.[10]

Officials decided there were only two situations where an immediate statement about the presence of a nuclear weapon would be unavoidable:

> If a bomb was lying within sight of the public, or if one had already exploded! If no explosion has occurred it is clearly undesirable to stimulate public interest in the crash by announcing that 'there is no danger of an atomic or high explosive detonation'. Until the appearance of such an announcement, the public would not necessarily imagine that any such danger had existed. If such an explosion had occurred ... it would obviously be necessary as soon as possible to make a statement.[11]

Washington diplomatically held its tongue and agreed to most of the proposed public relations plan, but they politely suggested that if American personnel were first on the scene they would obviously have the support of the British Government to ensure public safety.

Whatever was known in Whitehall about the Lakenheath crash, it was not until November 1979 that the local MP, Mr (later Sir) Eldon Griffiths, elicited a public statement from Francis Pym, the Secretary of State for Defence. Mr Griffiths asked:

> ... in view of the objections being made to the proposed deployment at United States bases in East Anglia of more modern nuclear weapons designed to prevent war, if he is satisfied with the safety arrangements at these and Royal Air Force airbases, taking into account incidents such as that which occurred in 1956 at RAF Lakenheath when burning fuel from

an aircraft may have come into close proximity to a bomb store containing nuclear weapons.

Eldon Griffiths' question was asked at a time when it had been suggested that American Cruise missiles might be deployed in the UK.[12]
The Secretary of State replied carefully that:

So far as the incident at Lakenheath in 1956 is concerned, the United States authorities have already stated that no nuclear materials were involved either within the crashed aircraft or in any buildings affected by the resulting fire. The storage of all nuclear weapons in the country is and will continue to be governed by standards prescribed by UK authorities, and I am entirely satisfied with our present arrangements. I can assure my honourable friend that storage arrangements are designed to reduce to the absolute minimum risk of damage to weapons by fires or other incidents and that nuclear weapons include safety features which make nuclear accidents virtually impossible and extreme precautions are taken. None the less, plans exist, and are exercised regularly, to protect the civil population from any hazard.[13]

That was not entirely the end of the matter because, in February 1958, eighteen months after the Lakenheath crash, a B-47 encountered engine problems on take-off from Greenham Common and released two drop-tanks containing jet fuel. The tanks burst into flames and the fire spread to a parked B-47 and to parts of a nearby hangar. The B-47 destroyed was one assigned to a Reflex mission, and it has been alleged that it had been loaded with a nuclear bomb. As a result, there were claims that the fire had caused increased levels of radiation on and around the airbase. Both the British and American authorities have consistently denied the involvement of nuclear weapons, but rumours persisted.[14]

In October 1996, both the Lakenheath and Greenham Common incidents were raised in the House of Commons. The Secretary of State for Defence, Mr Christopher Soames, reiterated the reply given in 1979 regarding the Lakenheath crash. On the incident at Greenham Common, he said that a copy of the official expurgated report on the incident had not been received from the American authorities until August 1996. Questioned on where the 'contaminated soil and aggregates' from Greenham Common, removed after the accident, had been stored, and what monitoring had subsequently taken place to ascertain whether toxic material hazardous to the environment had been released, Mr Soames said the incident had not given rise to any contaminated soil 'which would have required disposal in the manner suggested'. He added that he understood that debris from the accident was disposed of by the US authorities in accordance with routine procedures, as no special precautions were necessary.[15]

The Secretary of State went on:

> Due to public outcry from the 1961 report claiming an accident had taken place at Greenham Common, a radiation survey was subsequently undertaken by the University of Southampton Geosciences Advisory Unit, along with uranium measurements by the Isotope Geochemistry Unit. The survey using over 500 collected soil and humus samples showed no increase at Greenham Common over the presence of naturally occurring uranium.

The 1996 statement in Parliament failed to mention, however, another potential Broken Arrow incident that took place, also at Lakenheath, in January 1961. According to the official USAF report,[16] an F-100D aircraft, with a Mark 28 hydrogen bomb loaded on its centre line pylon, became involved in a fire when droppable fuel tanks were inadvertently released as it stood on its parking pad. The fire, it seems, was brought under control before the nuclear weapon was engulfed in flames or the heat set off the weapon's high explosives, and no nuclear reaction occurred. As soon as the fire was extinguished 'the weapon was found to be cool enough to be touched by bare hands, indicating the tritium bottle guillotine valve should not have been activated'. It took some time to offload the weapon and return it to the special weapons area. The report added that no contamination resulted. Other reports allege that the bomb was 'scorched and blistered' in the inferno.

Because the accident happened away from the scrutiny of the press and public on an operational base, neither the American Government nor the British would subsequently acknowledge that the accident ever happened. An official report from the American authorities accepted that the possibility of a nuclear accident releasing a cloud of plutonium which could threaten a large number of people 'was far from remote', and since most parts of western Europe, and particularly the UK, were more densely populated than many areas of the United States, such an accident would threaten the lives of a large number of people.

More alarming, however, is the fact that safety experts in the United States had identified a significant concern about the Mark 28 hydrogen bomb, Strategic Air Command's most widely deployed nuclear bomb. One of the bomb's internal cables was located close to the weapon's outer skin and, if the bomb was exposed to prolonged heat, the insulation of the cable could degrade, causing the wires inside it to short circuit. One of these wires was connected to the ready/safe switch, and another to the thermal battery that charged the X-unit. The consequence could be that a fire might actually arm a Mark 28, ignite its thermal battery, charge its X-unit and then detonate the high explosives. Depending on the particular model of the Mark 28, a blast anywhere from 70 kilotons to 1.5 megatons would immediately follow.

The Americans were realistic about the probability of an accidental nuclear weapon explosion. In 1955, the US Department of Defense commissioned a secret report entitled 'Acceptable Military Risks from Accidental Detonation of Atomic Weapons'. It compared the frequency of natural disasters in the United States – devastating earthquakes, floods and tornadoes – and tried to equate the probability of a nuclear weapon detonating as a result of an accident. The report suggested that the acceptable probability of a thermo-nuclear or hydrogen bomb detonation was one in 100,000 in the course of a year. The comparative acceptable risk of an atomic explosion was calculated as one in 125. Inevitably, those so-called 'acceptable risks' were kept from the public.[17]

Britain's Ministry of Defence was no less open than its American counter-parts in giving details of mishaps with nuclear weapons. In 2003 the MOD was forced to publish a list of twenty incidents with nuclear weapons between 1960 and 1991, following criticism from the parliamentary ombudsman.[18] Initially, Whitehall blocked a request and deflected queries under freedom of information legislation. However, the parliamentary ombudsman found the MOD guilty of maladministration, dismissed the objections of civil servants and ruled that disclosure would not endanger national security.

Among the twenty incidents disclosed was the denting of a nuclear weapon at RAF Marham, Norfolk, when it fell off a work stand in 1988, and the dropping of a nuclear bomb at RAF Honington in Suffolk when it was being loaded onto a V-bomber in 1976. The MOD insist that none of the UK incidents led to radiation leaks. 'There has never been an occurrence involving a British nuclear weapon which represented a threat to public safety or to the safety of service personnel,' an MOD spokesman stated.

NOTES

1 *Omaha World-Herald*, 11 June 1979.
2 Hansard, 9 November 1979.
3 Declassified telex from General Walsh, Commander 7th Air Division, South Ruislip, to General Curtis LeMay, Commander, Strategic Air Command, Offutt, Nebraska, 27 July 1956, from 'LeMay Papers', Library of Congress.
4 Campbell, Duncan, *The Unsinkable Aircraft Carrier: American Military Power in Britain* (London: Michael Joseph, 1984), p. 52.
5 Maggelet, Michael H., and James C. Oskins, *Broken Arrow: The Declassified History of US Nuclear Weapons Accidents*, lulu.com, 2007.
6 Department of Defense, Aircraft Accident Report, AF Form 14 (declassified).
7 Maggelet and Oskins, *Broken Arrow*, p. 83.
8 Schlosser, Eric, *Command and Control* (London: Allen Lane, 2013).
9 'UK hid nuclear accident threat', BBC News, 24 July 2003.
10 *Ibid.*
11 *Ibid.*
12 Hansard, 9 November 1979.
13 *Ibid.*
14 Maggelet and Oskins, *Broken Arrow*, pp. 271–77.
15 Hansard, 14 October 1996.
16 Declassified Air Munitions Letter, No. 136-11-56G, p. 28 (declassified from Secret Restricted Data Atomic Energy Act 1954).
17 Schlosser, *Command and Control*.
18 *Guardian*, 13 October 2003.

10

'WHO IS WATCHING THE PEOPLE WHO ARE WATCHING OUR NUKES?'

IN 1958, AN incident happened at the huge American airbase at Sculthorpe, near Fakenham in Norfolk, which had repercussions throughout the US military. The base was held hostage by an active-duty master sergeant, who locked himself inside a nuclear bomb store and threatened to cause an explosion by placing a .45 calibre pistol to the warhead of a nuclear bomb. It was eight hours before the sergeant was 'talked down' from his ultimate threat – eight hours during which Sculthorpe was in virtual lockdown.

Lt Col Henry Brinkman, of the US Army War College, recalls the highly classified meeting at the Pentagon which was set up as a direct result of the Norfolk threat, the first time in the US military that an incident of such seriousness involving nuclear weapons had occurred.[1] Brigadier General B.C. Harrison came straight to the point as he strode into the meeting: 'Gentlemen, we have a problem,' he began, before explaining exactly what had happened on the USAF's largest base in Europe.

What had taken place at Sculthorpe was hushed up at the time. It appears that even the British Government was not told the full story. A military personnel researcher, Eli Flyer, who attended the Pentagon meeting, said there was deep concern that, if the true story had been revealed, the consequences for the US could have been disastrous. 'Disclosure of the event would certainly have knocked us out of England,' he said, and England was 'the keystone to the US nuclear strategy in Europe at the time'.[2] It was not until 1962 that the true facts became known and, by then, a system had been developed and spread across the whole of the US military to prevent any similar problem ever happening again.

In the aftermath of the event, there was some dispute within the Pentagon about what would have happened in Norfolk if the sergeant had, in fact, fired his weapon. At a minimum, it was agreed, the impact of the bullet in all likelihood would have detonated the considerable amount of high explosives contained in the bomb, scattering nuclear debris into the atmosphere. Atomic bombs were not stored with their nuclear cores in situ to avoid an accidental nuclear detonation, but they still contained a small amount of nuclear material. Nevertheless, the possible consequences of nuclear hijack were considerable and the US was determined not to run the risk again.

The solution reached by the Pentagon inquiry was termed PRP, the Personnel Reliability Program. It was designed to screen tens of thousands of personnel who had access to the country's nuclear arsenal. The object was to guarantee only 'competent, stable, and dependable individuals' were approved to work with nuclear weapons. In the case of the master sergeant at Sculthorpe, it was quickly established that the man was being treated by a psychiatrist for serious depression, but that this had not barred him from working with nuclear weapons.

At the height of the Cold War an average of 100,000 American service personnel were screened, and passed the PRP programme. During the process candidates had to undergo a medical assessment and an in-depth interview. The candidate's personnel file was reviewed, and military investigators conducted an extensive background check to examine the candidate's professional, educational and personal history. But there were still gaps. Critics complained there was no routine or ongoing psychological testing, and that a candidate's entire medical evaluation might be limited to an examination of old medical records.

Once certified under PRP to work with nuclear weapons, personnel who later displayed suspect traits or personality disorders could be decertified, and many were, throughout the Cold War years. A worrying trend was that a number of PRP-approved personnel went on to commit suicide or serious crimes. The system was far from foolproof. Some individuals who passed the test were later found guilty of crimes ranging from rape to murder. An overall decertification rate of 3–4 per cent of those approved to work with nuclear weapons grew to be an issue of some concern.

Herbert L. Adams, an expert in PRP at Stanford University's Center for International Security and Co-operation, called on the Pentagon to strengthen the process by requiring a physician to examine all candidates using standard psychological testing, and improved post-approval monitoring.[3]

The ramifications of what happened at Sculthorpe had an impact throughout all the US military services. In the view of the Pentagon, PRP cut the risks of a similar incident where a mentally disturbed person could hold an entire base to ransom.

However, a question still remains as to whether the US authorities were entirely honest with the British Government at the time. In December 1962, when the full story emerged, questions were asked in Parliament about the Anglo-American Agreement governing the control of nuclear weapons kept at USAF bases in the United Kingdom.[4] Tom Driberg, a Labour MP, questioned what information the prime minister – then Harold Macmillan – had been given about the incident at Sculthorpe, 'when a mentally deranged master sergeant threatened to explode an atom bomb'. 'Was the prime minister satisfied', he asked, 'that United States personnel who hold positions of responsibility regarding control of nuclear or atomic weapons at US bases in the UK are medically examined as suitable in all respects for such responsibility?'

The prime minister played down the incident, and replied that the American serviceman referred to had 'locked himself in a shed for eight hours. The anxiety was not that he might explode an atomic bomb – there were none – but that he might do something foolish with a pistol. I do not think it necessary to consult the President of the United States about this,' he said, to laughter.

Mr Driberg persisted, saying that the Americans had now admitted that, whether it was an atomic bomb or not, it was an atomic or nuclear device that the master sergeant had threatened to destroy. Could the prime minister say whether there was any consultation at the time with Her Majesty's Government before false information was given to the press?

The prime minister replied that the sergeant, suffering from some mental delusions, shut himself in a shed and threatened to kill himself with a revolver. 'It is true there was some explosive in the building and it is just conceivable that he might have caused it to explode had he carried out his threat, but his threat was to kill himself, not shoot the explosive. There was no fissionable material in the building and no possibility of a nuclear explosion of any kind.'

Michael Foot stated that the information the prime minister had just given to the House, and the information that was given to Parliament four years previously, was contradicted in almost every particular by statements which had appeared on the authority of the United States in the last few days. He wanted the prime minister, before he landed himself into further absurdities, to reconsider the whole question and give a truthful statement.

The prime minister was not to be deterred. He said he was satisfied that his statement was correct, a true account of what had been said four years ago and of what had been said by the American authorities recently. It left questions hanging in the air, but undoubtedly what happened at Sculthorpe in 1958 had a deep impact on senior officers in the Pentagon, and changed the attitude of the American forces to the whole question of 'who was watching the people who watched the nukes'.

Seven years after the exchanges in Parliament over the Sculthorpe affair, fears of further unauthorised use of nuclear weapons by the Americans were again voiced in the Commons. This time, however, the questions surrounded the theft of an aircraft from the American airbase at Mildenhall in May 1969.

I remember the incident well. At the time I was news editor at Anglia Television. A phone call came into the newsroom from an informant at Mildenhall, asking if we were aware that an aircraft was missing from the Suffolk base and that the USAF was tracking it with growing concern. Gradually the story began to emerge that a young USAF mechanic, the holder of a medal for service in Vietnam, had stolen the four-engine transport aircraft, in the early hours of the morning, in an apparent attempt to fly solo back to the States. A few hours earlier, the 23-year-old airman, Sgt Paul Meyer, had been put to bed by a fellow sergeant, homesick and the worse for drink.

The C130 Hercules was tracked by radar, flying over Kent, passing out to sea near Brighton and heading for the Brest Peninsula. The aircraft was then set on a course that would have taken it out over the Atlantic. At that point the radar contact was lost. There is strong evidence that the USAF scrambled fighter aircraft to intercept the missing plane, and that the pilot of an F100 fighter jet spotted the C130 west of the Isle of Wight. The F100 pilot had difficulty in keeping contact due to the C130's slower speed and finally lost visual sight of the transport plane due to bad weather and significant cloud cover. It also appears that Meyer was taking evasive action to lose the shadowing fighter.

An embarrassed USAF spokesman later revealed that ships had been asked to search the area where the C130 was last seen, but it was unlikely any trace of the missing aircraft would be found before a full air search was mounted. Meyer, it transpired later, had contacted USAF authorities on the plane's radio shortly after his unauthorised take-off from Mildenhall. He requested a telephone hook-up with his wife in Virginia, where she lived with their three children, and refused to speak to any authorities on the ground.

According to a report in the St Petersburg Times,[5] Meyer told his wife that he was having trouble with the aircraft's automatic pilot. As he spoke to his wife, he said: 'Leave me alone for about five minutes, I've got trouble.' That was his last transmission. There were no further radar contacts and no other radio transmissions. US officials assumed that the C130 crashed into the sea. They told the American press the aircraft would not have had sufficient fuel to fly much further. However, the Pentagon said, in an official statement, that the aircraft would have had enough fuel in its tanks for a thirteen-hour flight.

The C130 Hercules had been widely used as a transport aircraft in Vietnam, and normally required a crew of five. Meyer had piloted light aircraft and, because of his job as a crew chief, was thoroughly familiar with the Hercules. He had often taxied Hercules transports at Mildenhall as part of his duties. He had also been allowed by some of the Hercules pilots to fly the C130, and had amassed quite a few hours' 'stick time' in this way. When he had started the engines he radioed that he was taking the aircraft to a remote hard standing for an engine test, but when taxiing it he promptly turned onto the active runway, opened the throttles and took off.

Meyer's home base was Langley Air Force Base in Virginia, and he had been in Suffolk on a 120-day mission. He was due to return to the States in thirty days. The Air Force admitted that he had been drinking in a public house off base the night before he stole the aircraft.

Rumours persisted at both Mildenhall and Lakenheath, the neighbouring base in Suffolk where the USAF had F100 fighters stationed, that the US authorities had scrambled jets with orders to shoot the C130 down. This may well have been true. The US military could not risk an American aircraft crashing on foreign territory, possibly in a populated area. Some American airmen, who later happened to be at the US base at Rhein Main in Germany, from where a reclamation team was sent to recover wreckage of the Hercules, claimed that parts of the aircraft washed up on the French coast were full of holes resembling bullet strikes, but this has never been confirmed. Another story suggested that when the F100s returned to Lakenheath, their guns were reloaded with ammunition, and airmen who carried out the reloading were ordered not to talk about it.

The most likely theory about what happened was published in a book called *Ghosts of the Air* by Martin Caidin.[6] He suggested that Meyer lost control of the Hercules and the aircraft became inverted, the result of an inexperienced pilot putting the aircraft into a steep bank.

The incident raised concerns in Parliament on 25 June 1969,[7] and a defence minister was forced to explain that it would be altogether a mistake to conclude that anything remotely comparable could have occurred 'with an aircraft possessing a nuclear capability'. He was pressed by one MP to commission an inquiry in order to ascertain the extent of the risks involved, given the presence of United States nuclear bases in the UK. The minister, John Morris, replied that there were very elaborate procedures in place to ensure that there was no possibility of the unauthorised use of nuclear weapons, but it would not be in the public interest to describe those procedures in detail.

MPs were still not satisfied, and appeared to believe that the USAF had indeed shot down the Hercules. On 24 July, Prime Minister Harold Wilson was asked by Tom Driberg MP, in relation to the 'recent removal and destruction of an aircraft from Mildenhall and the danger to British people thus caused, would he seek to co-ordinate a study of the implications of this incident with particular reference to the anti-radar device with which this aircraft was equipped and the method by which it was destroyed'.[8]

The prime minister refused to add to what had already been said about the incident the previous month. So the question of whether Sgt Meyer crashed, or was shot down, remains unanswered.

The same year that the USAF base at Sculthorpe was placed on lock-down, and virtually held hostage by an armed and mentally unstable master sergeant threatening to fire at stored nuclear weapons, there was another incident, this time at the American airbase at Alconbury near Huntingdon. On 13 June 1958, an airman mechanic with no flight training stole a B-45 Tornado bomber, taking off down the airbase's main runway just after midnight. What his objective or motive might have been will never be known, but fortunately the aircraft, which was capable of carrying a nuclear weapon, was not armed. Three minutes after take-off the aircraft crashed, its wreckage blocking the main Edinburgh–London railway line at Abbot's Ripton. Airman Second Class Vernon L. Morgan was killed instantly. A USAF inquiry took place, but the details of how a sophisticated aircraft could be taken by an unauthorised airman, from under the noses of the base security, were never publicly released.

NOTES

1   Lt Col Henry D. Brinkman, US Army War College, 'The History of the Nuclear Weapon Personnel Reliability Programme', April 2000.
2   *Ibid.*
3   *Ibid.*
4   Hansard, 6 December 1962.
5   *St Petersburg Times; Sarasota Herald Tribune.*
6   Caidin, Martin, *Ghosts of the Air* (London: Bounty Books, 2005).
7   Hansard, 25 June 1969.
8   *Ibid.*, 24 July 1969.

BIBLIOGRAPHY

Alibek, Ken, with Stephen Handelman, *Biohazard: The Chilling True Story of the Largest Covert Biological Weapons Programme in the World* (New York: Random House, 1999).

Bowyer, Michael J.F., *Force for Freedom: The USAF in the UK since 1948* (Yeovil: Patrick Stephens, 1994).

Boyes, John, *Project Emily: Thor IRBM and the RAF* (Stroud: Tempus, 2008).

Braithwaite, Sir Rodric, *Across the Moscow River* (New Haven: Yale University Press, 2002).

Brinkman, Lt Col Henry D., 'The History of the Nuclear Weapon Personnel Reliability Programme' (US Army War College, April 2000).

Caidin, Martin, *Ghosts of the Air* (London: Bounty Books, 2005).

Campbell, Duncan, T*he Unsinkable Aircraft Carrier: American Military Power in Britain* (London: Michael Joseph, 1984).

Catterall, Peter (ed.), *The Macmillan Diaries II: 1957–1966* (London: Macmillan, 2011).

Cocroft, Wayne D. & Roger J.C. Thomas, *Cold War Building for Nuclear Confrontation* (London: English Heritage, 2003).

Dalton, Mark, *The Royal Observer Corps Underground Monitoring Posts* (Bradford upon Avon: Folly Books, 2011).

Grant, Matthew, *After the Bomb: Civil Defence and Nuclear War in Britain* (Basingstoke: Palgrave Macmillan, 2010).

Hall, R. Cargill, 'The Truth About Overflights' (*US Military Quarterly*, 1997).

Heazell, Paddy, *Most Secret: The Hidden History of Orford Ness* (Stroud: The History Press, 2010).

Hoffman, David E., *The Dead Hand: Reagan, Gorbachev and the Untold Story of the Cold War Arms Race* (London: Icon Books, 2011).

Maggelet, Michael H., and James C. Oskins, *Broken Arrow: The Declassified History of US Nuclear Weapons Accidents* (lulu.com, 2007).

Portanova, Dr Peter L., and Dr L. Parker Temple, 'Project Emily and Thor IRBM in the UK', *Air Power History*, September 2009.

Randles, Jenny, *From Out of the Blue* (New Brunswick, New Jersey: Global Communications, 1991).

Reed, Thomas C., *At the Abyss: An Insider's History of the Cold War* (New York: Random House, 2004).

Ross DFC, Wg Cdr A.E. (ed.), *Through Eyes of Blue: Personal Memories of the RAF 1918–2001* (Shrewsbury: Airlife Publishing, 2002).

Schlosser, Eric, *Command and Control* (London: Allen Lane, 2013).

Twigge, Stephen & Len Scott, *Planning Armageddon: Britain, the United States and the Command of Western Nuclear Forces 1945–1964* (Amsterdam: Harwood Academic Publishers, 2000).

Watson, Brian, *Some Kind of Club: The History of ROC Group Six* (Norfolk: No. 6 Group ROC, 1984).

Wynn, Humphrey, *RAF Nuclear Deterrent Forces* (London: HMSO, 1994).

INDEX

Morgan, Airman 2nd Class
  Vernon L. 154
Morris, Derek 54, 55, 58
Morris, John 154
Moscow 24, 25, 67
Murphy-Dean Agreement
  18, 19
NASA (National Space
  Agency) 139
National Archives (TNA)
  31, 97
National Trust 13
NATO 46, 101, 115, 139
NBC (Nuclear, Biological &
  Chemical) 119
NHS 94
Norfolk & Norwich Hospital
  126
Norfolk 12–15, 21, 34, 48,
  71, 73, 96, 118, 121,
  127, 129, 147, 150
Norfolk Fire Service 103
North Walsham 66
Northern Line 123
Norwich 93, 99, 115, 118,
  121–26
Norwich City Fire Brigade 103
Norwich City Police 122
Norwich Evening News 126
Nottingham RSG 93
Nuclear Bombs:
  Blue Danube: 41–44, 48,
    49, 51, 53–56, 59,
    60, 63
  Blue Steel: 63
  Mark 3: 15
  Mark 4: 15
  Mark 6: 140–42
  Mark 28: 146, 147
  Red Beard: 43, 53, 54,
    60, 62
  WE 177: 44, 64
  Violet Club: 43, 44
  Yellow Sun: 44, 64
Nuclear Missiles:
  Blue Streak: 68, 76, 77, 78
  Cruise: 16, 19, 145
  Jupiter: 66, 75, 76
  Minuteman: 76
  Polaris: 14, 45, 64, 78
  SS-20: 16, 19
  Thor: 12, 14, 18, 19, 48,
    67–70, 72–78
  Titan: 76, 78
Observer Newspaper 133
Official Secrets Act 49, 50
Old Catton 109
Omaha World Herald 141

Operation Buffalo 42
Operation Ju-Jitsu 26, 30
Operation Robin 34
Orford Ness 14, 39, 40–45,
  96, 129, 130–32, 134,
  136–39
Oskins, James C. 142
OTH (Over the Horizon)
  129, 131, 134, 138
Paris Arms Control
  Conference 34
Parry, Wyn 126
Pasechnik, Vladimir 120
Penney, Dr William 39
Pentagon 142, 149–53
Peripheral 93
Pincher, Chapman 134
Pirelli 68
Plesetsk 131
Poland 33
Portanova, Dr Peter L. 71, 74
Porton Down 118, 122–25,
  127
Powers, Gary 34
Project 440-L 129
Project 441-L 129
Project 'E' Weapons: 56
Project Emily 66–68, 71, 74
Protect & Survive 11, 115, 116
Provost Branch 60
PRP (Personal Reliability
  Programme) 150, 151
Pym, Francis 140, 144
Quarry 95, 92
Queen Elizabeth I 97, 98
Quick Readiness Alert
  (QRA) 12
Radiac Survey Meter (RSM)
  111
RAF Air Defence Museum 104
RAF Bases:
  Barnham 14, 48–54, 56–64
  Bawburgh 77, 100–04
  Bawdsey 96, 130, 135
  Cottesmore 64
  Coltishall 96
  Duxford 77
  Faldingworth 49, 51, 59,
    63, 64
  Feltwell 14, 48, 71, 74,
    96, 129, 130
  Finningly 64
  Fylingdales 15, 129
  Honington 48–60, 64, 96,
    110, 147
  Horsham St Faiths 110
  Marham 17, 39, 48, 49,
    51, 96, 147

Mepal 48, 72
Neatishead 96, 101, 103,
  104, 115
North Pickenham 48,
  72–74
Scampton 39
Shepherd's Grove 48, 72
Swanton Morely 124
Tuddenham 48, 71, 72
Upwood 23
Waddington 39, 49
Wattisham 96, 110, 113
Watton 34, 72
West Raynham 23, 96
Wittering 14, 41, 43, 49,
  51, 56, 60, 96
Wyton 32, 34, 96
RAF Regiment 64
Randell, Ron 63
Reading 62
Reagan, President Ronald
  139
Red Star 30
Reed, Thomas S.C. 31,
  33–35
Reeve, Flt Lt 32
Regional Commissioner
  (East Anglia) 96–100
Regional Commissioner 16,
  91, 94, 95, 97
Regional Seats of
  Government (RSG) 94
Rendlesham Forest 138, 139
Robathan, Stuart 53–55
ROC (Royal Observer Corps)
  17, 106–08, 115, 116
ROC No 6 Group 107–09
ROC Group Headquarters:
  Bedford 110
  Colchester 110
  Norwich 107, 109, 110,
    113, 114
  Lincoln 110
ROC Headquarters, Bentley
  Priory 110
ROC Sector Control 109
Rolls Royce 52
Rotor 77, 100–02
Royal Engineers 72
Royal Flying Corps 41
Royal Warrant 97
RP1 Kerosene 70, 73
Rudasill, Bob 136–38
Russia 24–27, 29, 34, 40,
  100
Russian Spy Trawlers 46
SACEUR (Supreme Allied
  Commander Europe) 40

Visit our website and discover thousands of other History Press books.

www.thehistorypress.co.uk